CHAPTER ONE CHILDHOOD

The morning was bright and sunny. Felici
what was happening. Daddy was coming
where they went each day to collect the m
missed the run for two reasons, one she loved the spin in the new car her dad had just got, a Morris Minor his first car and secondly, she loved to bottle feed the pet lamb that Mrs Ferry the milk woman was rearing. The lamb's mother had gotten killed by a car so Felicity had great respect for the dangers of the road and of cars but she loved to tinker with the gears, brakes etc. when her parents came home from school where they both taught. She actually succeeded in getting the brake off at one stage and ended up in a river at the end of the garden. Felicity was an only child born in 1943 to parents who were considered old, relevant to the times that were in it. They were both teachers from large families. They were teaching in schools thirty miles apart and only got together on vacations and then only by depending on public transport which was anything but efficient. Because her parents were working so far apart Felicity was sent to her grannies to be reared where she was in charge of her Aunty Bridget whom she christened Bushy. She was aptly named as she had a head of bushy hair and was a big loving soul who did not know how to be cross with a child. Granny was a gentle old lady all dressed in long black clothes which was the fashion of the time. Granny always had a welcome for travellers. They were treated with respect, put sitting by the fire and given a mug of tea and bread. Their accents and modus operandi were different from the settled folks and they bestowed a blessing on the family when they were leaving the house. She found it strange that granny insisted on scalding the cup they drank out of, easier to understand now when you think how rampant tuberculosis was at that time. The home was what is now referred to as a bungalow, located off the road with a lake at its edge. It had three bedrooms, a kitchen, and a sitting room that no one got into except visitors, and it had the proverbial china cabinet containing the china and glasses, which were never used. The toilet was outside, like most of the other houses. There was no running water or electricity, so the oil lamp was lit every night to give light. It was here that her granny, whom she christened Dya, lived with her daughter Bushy and her son Anthony, and

during the winter, her son Jim, who did seasonal work in Scotland. It was a lovely, very quiet place with helpful neighbours, and there was shared help saving hay and cutting the turf for winter fuel. Granny's family was poor, the father was a butcher that could not make ends meet so he also took the road to Scotland each summer to supplement the household budget and Granny took in sewing. There was a veil of secrecy surrounding the father and rumour had it that he had a romantic encounter in Scotland and that he committed suicide, a fact that Felicity was never able to clarify. His name was never mentioned, and he is buried in a separate grave with another sibling. These people were gentle folk who looked out for one another and took on each other's worries. Felicity retained a deep gra for the small house at the edge of the lake with water holes in the rocks, blueberries in the heather, hens in their warm nests, the cat, the dog, the donkey and the one cow, all one big happy family. Uncle Anthony with treats in his pocket and the neighbours dropping in and out. One of her memories was bad thunder and lightning and her uncle Jim out in the middle of the night trying to get the cow and the donkey in from the field. While she was cosy beside her Aunty Bushy in the bed off the kitchen. Her uncle Anthony worked in the labour exchange in Dunloe and was Felicity's main man to find birds' nests, carry her to see the eggs or the baby birds and give shoulder rides. Anthony liked his beer too much leaving him out of favour with Bushy and Granny. In order to give him a fright one night on his way home they dressed this tall neighbour up as a ghost in a white sheet, made and stitched by Granny, who jumped out at him coming home. He went screaming with fright towards the house. It was said that not a drop of alcohol passed his lips for three months. There was great excitement one weekend as her parents were going to a wedding and Felicity was also invited. They arrived in their best outfits and were delighted to see their daughter so happy. Mother had bought her nice new shoes. She had her bath in front of the fire and was all dolled up in her finery. Mother went off to get ready while Felicity struggled with the new shoes to get them off and succeeded in getting one off which she immediately threw into the fire, discovered too late to be rescued. Apart from the waste it was a real disaster as money was very scarce. The highlight of Felicity's life was trips to the local town in the buggy where they would visit relatives and were sure to get a cup of tea and biscuits. Aunty Bushy would say we do not want anything to eat but Felicity would turn around and say, "but is that not what we came for". There were three children at the cousins and Felicity loved to play with them and was really thrilled if it was bath time and they were all three in the bath in front of the fire usually on a Saturday evening. It was a happy relaxed existence with neighbours helping neighbours, visitors coming and going, and plenty of hard work tilling the land and cutting timber to keep the fires burning which was the main way of cooking. Granny had another daughter named Rose who worked in Dublin and came sometimes. She was a single lady who did not understand children. She used to get cross with Felicity for not eating her dinner and one day there was quite a row, so Felicity went off and climbed into a hen's nest and refused to answer any of the calls. As the house was near the lake everyone was frantic out looking for her including all the neighbours, but no amount of searching could unearth her. Eventually, she had to do a wee and emerged whereupon Aunty Rose gave her a slap on the hand, her first slap ever and she never forgot it. Felicity was surrounded by love and undivided attention. It is a proven psychological fact that love is the single most important attribute in a child's life to give a well-rounded happy person. Granny died when Felicity was still in the house and she remembers all the people coming to the house, the crying and the endless cups of tea and drink for the men. She was sad and crying too but no one headed her or tried to comfort her as it was presumed that a child of two and a half would not understand. She remembers being left with strangers when they took Granny away and that she never came back. Grannys passing was a sad, mysterious time for Felicity leaving a great void in the house which was lonely and was fearful when she seemed to be ignored in the general upheaval. She quickly learned that questions on Granny's whereabouts were not welcome, even causing her precious Bushy to cry so she sunk into the wall of silence surrounding her absence. How much better it is now when people explain to children what has happened. As Felicity was born at the end of world war two her mother just avoided the ban on married women working after they got married. Her parents taught in different schools a distance apart and had no transport except the push bicycle and tried to get to see Felicity as often as they could.

Her father was from a family of seventeen, fourteen of whom survived. The grandfather was a teacher who put the whole family on for teaching whether they liked it or not. His theory was that they would be educated and they could do what they liked after that. There is a special desk in St Pats training college with their surname on it. Her father hated teaching but was stuck with it for the rest of his life as were several of the other siblings. Felicity's mother had been paid for to go to training college by an Uncle who was married and lived near Lough Eske but had no children. Felicity and her parents would often visit him in his big house and he would give Felicity's dad a glass of sherry which he hated so Felicity on one occasion grabbed it off her father when the Uncle had gone out and dumped it into the range where the flames almost hit the roof and there was ashes everywhere. Her father's family were well off, the father being a teacher, they had a post office and Granny was wealthy in her own right as her father was a linen merchant and a good businessman. He bought his daughter the house as a wedding present and it was the finest house in Teelin where they lived. The grandparents managed to go to the Canaries on holidays on one occasion, something that was unheard of at that time. It was a time that you were blessed if you could produce a big family. Out of the seventeen children, there were only five girls so it was a household of big strong men. They were friendly and visited each other but did not get too deeply involved in each other's lives. Locally it was known that the father was proud of his clutch and would appear at the local pub flanked by the clan and expect to be instantly served. Grandad was a tough disciplinarian and the story is told of the inspector visiting the school where the Grandfather was on his knees lighting the fire with the turf supplied by the children who had to bring in a few sods of turf each day for the fire. The inspector told Grandfather to remove his hat when he came in and was answered by saying yes when you remove yours first. He was reputed to be a great teacher and ran hedge schools when the English banned education, Grandfather was also into fishing from his boat, went hunting in the Dunlewey Mountains for deer and rabbits, and farmed a modest farm, all aimed at feeding the family. It is a credit to him that he raised a fine, upright family that never put a foot wrong except for one who went off to Dublin and was uncontactable. But Granny, who was a warrior, went to Dublin and searched the seedier areas of Dublin until she found him.

She took him back home, and he remained on the straight and narrow for the rest of his life. Maybe there is a lesson to be learned by the modern-day parent that strict discipline works. When the Grandfather visited Felicities Mum was a wreck having his dinner on the table at one o'clock sharp as requested by him. Saving turf was a national necessity done by practically every family. Going to the bog to work was considered a great day out and the sandwiches eaten on the bog tasted special. Bog holes were a constant danger for the younger children and there were reported fatalities thankfully not too often. The boys were got out of bed before going to school in the morning to set the fishing nets and lift lobster pots. You get a picture of solid hard-working people fishing, shooting, farming, saving turf and doing their normal job as well while enjoying life and making the most of it. When Felicity's parents managed to come at a weekend Felicity who normally slept with her Aunty was moved to her cot up in the guest room where she found it cold as she was used to sleeping in the bed with Bushy so she kept asking when they were going away, leaving them in no doubt that the sooner the better. This invariably led to tensions when mother questioned whether they were trying to turn her daughter against her parents. There was quite an uproar one weekend when they brought her a toy rubber soldier which she eyed with suspicion and declared in a loud voice "stick a pin in his arse". Where had she heard such a thing, and should they shift her to the other granny but eventually all settled and was serene again. Life was good in Granny's, she was the only child around, so she got donkey rides when the turf was being brought home, went bird nesting, got shoulder rides and was cock of the walk. As time passed and her parents found schools close to each other, they were able to rent a house and bring Felicity to live with them. Poor Bushy was heartbroken at Felicity's departure, and it was a two-way thing, leaving Felicity upset and unable to fully comprehend what or why she had to go. When she moved to her parent's house, she met a woman named Betty who lived with the family and who Felicity talked to and interacted with all day, so she became an important influence in her life, helping to prevent the loneliness of having no brothers or sisters and living in an isolated place. To get a suitable person to be a minder and live in the house with them, a second Mrs Duoubtfire, involved learning by word of mouth where there might be a suitable person, taking note that there were no phones or agencies, and people did not advertise so the social network was invaluable. A girl usually seventeen years plus from a poor backward area would be recruited to do the minding and the housework. After much searching, Betty was hired. Betty was strict and would insist that Felicity would sit in her chair until the floor that she had washed was dry. If Betty came with them in the car, she would push the front of the car going up a hill thinking that it might help to get it to the top of the hill. Felicity's parents were not home until after four o clock, so it was a long day for Felicity. Her parents left the wireless set for a child's story to come on at 2.15 pm and Felicity knew what button to press but it was followed by an agony aunts program and Felicity found this program also very interesting but never revealed that she was listening to it on a regular basis. As it kept her quiet Betty turned a deaf ear. Felicity invented a family for herself of two brothers and two sisters John, Jack, Nuala and Jane with whom she interacted, bossing them, teaching them, and putting them to sleep. She did not spare the rod on them if they did not behave. Contrary to what you might think, Felicity was never subjected to slaps or the rod, but books and the media had their influence. even then. They became very real to her and she talked about them incessantly but was wise enough to only do this to a chosen few and only in the family. This was an era when babies were left in the upstairs bedrooms protected from noise and stimulation contrary to modern advice, the mantra being that children should be seen but not heard. When children had to go to the hospital the parents were told not to visit as it only upset the child. It blows the mind to think of a two or three-year-old child being suddenly deserted, compounded by the fact that they were sick and miserable already and maybe in pain. Eating out, having coffee, leisure activities, spa treatments or swimming was unheard of for the ordinary punter. As time progressed, Felicity's family was able to graduate from renting to buying their first house for a thousand pounds, right across the road from the beach. In the summer, it was buzzing with visitors, but in the winter, it was bleak and quiet but never lonely with the constant crashing of the waves. Felicity remembers sitting in the car and listening to her parents discuss the pros and cons of buying the house and wondering if they could afford it. She had gone with them to another house beside her father's school, isolated in a mountainous area, and was very glad they did not get that one.

Life in the 1950s was a different time, harder but freer with issues like murder, rape, kidnapping and sexual abuse rarely if ever mentioned and so life was less tension-ridden, instead, money was scarce, transport difficult, heat, food, accommodation and medical care were the burning issues. Children were free to roam the countryside on foot or by bicycle as long as they were home at a certain time. Safety and kidnapping did not come into the equation. You got to Irish dancing if you could cycle or walk there and that was the total of the extracurricular activities provided. Wearing slacks was frowned on in the fifties. Mother assured Felicity that if she came home in a pair of slacks her father would throw a skirt out the window before she would be allowed in. This posed a problem as Felicity loved boating so she resolved to push her luck by cleaning the house from top to toe a day that her parents had gone visiting and cooking a nice meal, at the same time putting on the sinful slacks and waiting for their return, The parents came back, not a word was said much to her amazement and slacks were accepted from then on. Because Felicity suffered from a heart murmur her mother was over-protective of her and not at all keen to let her go swimming in the cold water. Felicity was no angel and managed to escape Betty's eagle eye and make her way to the beach and the lovely waves in the month of March. Unfortunately, mother was cycling home from school and found her daughter out in the waves so Betty got her walking papers. The long protracted tug of war between mother and daughter had begun and Betty departed which put the nail in the coffin as far as Felicity was concerned. It was not a time when any attempt was made to explain to a child the what and the why of life the result being animosities were built up and only really understood when the child became a parent herself. Mother was a disciplinarian. She was acutely aware of public opinion, shy, and house-proud. Needless to say, she and Felicity clashed, which led to many rows and frustrations for both parties. The fact that communication between a mother and child was hard only entrenched their differences over the years, causing a lot of unhappiness. Her father was a gentle giant as far as Felicity was concerned and she loved him dearly. He was sociable and liked a drink with his friends and would often recite poetry in the local hotel of an evening, his favourite being Dangerous Dan Mc Grew. He had many interests including his vegetable garden, his boat for fishing, and cutting timber in Ards forest to provide fuel for the winter. Father had an award-winning vegetable garden with potatoes, onions, carrots, peas, lettuce, beetroot and brussel sprouts which left them self-sufficient for the winter. He set peas and attended them lovingly to get the perfect peas, instead he was rewarded with sweet pea flowers much to the amusement of his wife and daughter. Fish were caught in the summer by fishing rods and long lines which had a hundred hooks which were set in the sandy bottoms baited with lugworm. They caught flat fish like plaice. Lug worms were dug out of the sand and were where the wiggly pattern appeared in the sand. The fish would then be cured by immersing them in brine to marinate and then drying them in the sun until they were bone dry. They will then be kept for the whole winter and were available in the shops. They were a stable diet on Fridays and were horrible. When it became time for Felicity to start school it was decided that she would go to her mother's school which was a two teachers school. Being a pupil where a parent teaches has its problems and Felicity couldn't wait to get into the master's room and away from her mother. In her mother's room, she insisted on sharing the desk with the girl who had the most nits and fleas in her hair and so began a battle of wits with a well-meaning mother who failed to persuade her to change desks. Every year Felicity and her dad would await the arrival of the cuckoo to see who would hear him first. Her mother would ask at school "up hands all who heard the cuckoo" and Felicity would wait impatiently running up and down to remind her to ask so she could put up her hand. Felicity progressed well but had to learn fast, and when the master's cane was burned, she was blamed as she and her mother were the last to leave the school as they had to wait to be collected by the dad. She got five slaps on both hands, which left a mark, but never said a word to her mother as, at that young age, she recognized the trouble it might cause between the two teachers, especially as she was innocent. She never held it against the master and visited him in his old age in the nursing home. He would sometimes give her a ride on the handlebars of his bicycle, as he lived near where their rented house was. The master who was called Eddie Cannon was a great teacher and loved to write his own plays which he then got the pupils to perform in the local hall. Felicity was good at maths and on getting all her sums right on her homework page the Master got suspicious and said he was sick of her parents doing her sums for her so he put her up to the front of

the class and made her do them again but she again got them all right as only stupid parents would do the sums for their child. She once again instinctively knew not to mention this little episode. There was a system in the school that the stairs and the playrooms had to be swept after the lunch break and whoever got the brushes first could do this job when the others were back in class. Because Felicity ate her lunch at school she got the two brushes and gave one to her so-called boyfriend who was a boy from the cottages and not at all acceptable to her mother who was confronted by the happy pair if she ventured out of the classroom. On the rare occasion, she even managed a smile. Felicity travelled each day to her mother's school and would arrive early as dad had to drop them off before proceeding on to Creeslough where he taught. Mother would drag Felicity off to mass after they were dropped while Felicity would dream of being up at the school playing football and even football was controversial as Felicity had nice leather fur-lined boots while the others had black hobnail boots which she coveted but was not allowed to get. Her main weapons that Felicity had to annoy her mother were not eating and not sleeping. She would sit up in the bed singing and for good measure adding the name of the undesirable boyfriend into the song. Poor mother would bake two dozen queen cakes as Felicity would only eat the crumbs off the paper when they were taken off the buns.
She loved messing with hair, and one morning she tied a large red bow on her father's hair. He rushed off to work, unaware that the bow was still there. Fortunately, he went in for the paper on his way and was duly warned by the astonished shopkeeper. Her mother was not pleased with Felicity's trick on her husband and warned her not to try it again.
Saturday mornings were relaxing, and Felicity would go to her parent's bed to snuggle down. This came to an end when she was eight. Her mother said she was too big and the bed was too small, but Felicity knew there was plenty of room in the bed. It simply added to her frustration with her mother and was seen as a further rejection.
Felicity, who loved dogs, wrote to her Aunt Rose, asking her to please get her a dog if she had enough money. She seemed to understand that money was scarce and should not be squandered at such a young age. In due course, a lovely white-haired dog arrived that she called Shaggy. He had one bad habit—running after sheep, and her dad used to give

him a beating, but the poor dog did not know what he was being beaten for. Shaggy was Felicity's faithful companion wherever she went.
Felicity had first cousins in Kiltimagh, two little girls called Ann and Nuala that she visited. They had a gentle loving mother that was not good at discipline and Felicity enjoyed herself so much that she did not want to come home. Eventually, it was a case of no surrender and the parents came halfway to collect her for home. In retrospect, she would say it was the company and the loving mother that appealed to Felicity coming from a one-child strict family. Felicity at this stage got her hands on a few books of dubious content as she had become an avid reader. They disappeared from under her pillow but Felicity managed to replace them and when she had read them left them in a prominent position where mother could see that she had won again. Felicity's father bought a small boat to fish lobsters and set nets during the summer and she loved to mess around in the boat. Lift lobster pots, take out her friends, and show off her expertise in handling it. On one occasion a large trawler came into the bay to shelter. The parents were away and Felicity brought three of her pals out to the trawler to investigate. It was a foreign trawler and the sailors invited them on board and showed them all over it. Father came back and was quickly informed where his daughter had gone so he had to borrow a boat and head out after them being well aware of the dangers. Luckily nothing adverse had happened.
It was a time of great freedom. Felicity and her pals, three other little girls Angela, Rosaleen and Ann formed a club which they called the famous four modelled on Enid Blyton's famous five. They sourced an old shed close by, an easy acquisition among the many holiday homes deserted in the winter. So numerous they presented a challenge to see how many they could break into which proved to be over fifty per cent. The idea that this could be construed as breaking and entering never entered their heads and once achieved was promptly abandoned. They held meetings once a week and collected the women's own magazines to read the agony columns and see if there were any hidden words of wisdom that would clarify love, sex, and babies for them. Their knowledge was a little advanced when they discovered an old man who had no bathroom and would come out to relieve himself, not realising that there were peeping toms behind the hedge. It got quite boring after two or three times, and anyway, the waiting was tedious. Her best friend was Angela Walsh who

lived in the local hotel that her parents ran and was the hub of the local area's activities. In Angela's house, the mother was very strict and treated all visiting kids as her own which would sometimes involve a prod in the back to sit up straight at the table and eat your food silently, say please and thank you and you ate what you got whether you liked it or not. Felicity hated soft eggs and could only swallow them by covering the yellow with some other food and thinking about a special food that she liked and pretending it was this food. Mrs Walsh was a very busy woman and sometimes she would lose the run of herself like the time she had English visitors, a captain and his wife and son. She declared in the kitchen that she did not know why they were delaying. I think you invited them to dinner. Angela and Felicity were duly dispatched to the local shop for the proverbial cheese and ham and they were eventually fed. Mullins was the local and only shop in the area run by three unmarried siblings and they would let you in any time of the day if you wanted something. They were the local post office, estate agents, director of tourists, stockist of fish from the local fishermen, protector of luggage, parcels and even would mind your car if you were going away. They were no friend of children as they informed the parents if they felt you were buying inappropriate stuff. As they were a permanent fixture they were utterly reliable. Gossip was part of their lives and who could blame them for looking for distractions? Theirs was a life of supply and demand, of gossip, friendship, and even advice. Felicity loved going to Angela's house to play after school, where there was plenty of company, and although it was half a mile away, there was no problem cycling off on your own with the proviso to be home at six p.m. Felicity will never forget watching "Quatermass," a terrifying film, and having to walk home in the dark after. She can relive it still by closing her eyes. One must remember that there were no mobile phones, not even house phones, so there was no one to call even if you were in dire straits. Angela's parents were one of the first in the area to get a TV, and it was magic to Felicity and her friends. Angela had two older brothers who were duly told the facts of life at a certain age by their father and were eagerly waited on by the girls to hear the gory details. Their sex education left a lot to be desired as the descriptions were often mysterious leaving one more confused than ever. After the brothers had the chat about the birds and the bees with their father they were not much further on as how could you question a man who was stuttering and using big words they had never heard before and being bright red with embarrassment. One of the brothers had a story about top-secret events involving humans and animals having intercourse and the female producing offspring that were half animal and half human. This brother said there was a special institution where they were all housed and if you lived near it you could hear these strange sounds coming from it at night. Felicity had been informed about periods but when she told Angela's brothers they said it was a mad Felicity story, the same brother that came to Felicity's birthday party and her mother served soup but as it was a green colour he told everyone that it was pea soup and not to drink it, leaving mother mystified why no one liked the soup. During the long winter days, the famous four were keen to try smoking so they got a packet of cigarettes in the local shop, never thinking that the information would be passed on to the parents. When mother asked her about cigarettes she said it was sweet cigarettes but that was the end of that adventure. Each Christmas Angela's parents would bring Angela and her friends to Derry to see the pantomime. Felicity had her little ball of money to give to Mrs Walsh for the tickets which she always refused. They were brought to a restaurant before the show and given a menu, it was Felicity's first time being presented with a menu and she had no clue what to get. It was a magnificent learning curve and gave a glance into another world. Felicity cooked scrambled eggs for Mrs Walsh and her mum when they were doing their yearly collection for St Vincent De Paul and was so proud when Mrs Walsh said it was the best scramble eggs she ever ate. Next door to Felicity were two holiday bungalows belonging to two related families from Co Tyrone who had five and three children. They became firm friends over the years and as Felicitys parents were on the spot, they kept an eye on the houses during the winter. Felicity's mother was not too impressed when she heard that they would put visiting children out during family meal time including her precious Felicity who learned not to divulge too much information to mum and prayed that no blow-up would occur between the families. Later in life, Felicity could see the sense in keeping other children out during family mealtime especially when it was a big family. As regards the area, they not alone lived in a vibrant seaside resort but had a beautiful lake surrounded by mountains called Seissagh Lake. It was around this time that they found a cave in one of the hills and sought the help of Amber, a brown Labrador belonging to Angela to explore it. As they would get their clothes dirty they explored it in their slips with torches. It was deep and wonderful and equated with the famous five books which told of many wonderful adventures had by them. Eventually, Felicity's dad got wind of what was going on and came to investigate. To his horror discovered it was a badger's den they had been exploring. It does not bear thinking about what would have happened if the badger had young pups.

They made friends with a local butcher who allowed them in while he was dissecting the animals in preparation for the shop, again not mentioned at home as it might sound a bit bloodthirsty and anyway parents had funny ideas. As the animals were already dead it did not bother them in the slightest to watch the gruesome dissections, but on another level, they knew not to discuss it with the adults. Mother had a strict rule about being back home at six o'clock sharp and Felicity remembers the slaps she got on both hands when she was late. Because Felicity was a bad eater, this gave mother lots of grief so she was summoned each day from the beach at 11 am for a bowl of porridge which she hates with a passion to this day. Her memories of this time included her father being on the beach with her when she was much younger making sand castles and later teaching her how to swim. She does not remember her mother ever being on the beach but then again she does not remember any of the other mums on the beach so maybe it was not the done thing. It certainly was not a time when mothers were to be found sunbathing and neither were continental holidays ever mentioned. Felicity will recall the big deal it was if you had to go to England for a funeral, then again there was no Ryanair and fares were greatly inflated.

CHAPTER TWO ADOLESCENCE

The focus of life revolved around the Portnablagh Hotel where her best friend Angela lived. In the evening they would attend the dances in the ballroom. Felicity had an uncle, Brendan, who was single and used to spend the summers with them. He was friendly with one of the barmaids and was given the task of escorting Felicity home preferably before midnight. He had a willing ear and a ready answer to Felicity's questions. Questions of life, love, relationships, people and how to get her parents to realise that she was no longer a child. He would often end up pushing her into the side of the road on the way home as it was narrow and busy with cars and she was unaware of the dangers of cars at night. His caring nature saved the parents from collecting her at night and it suited Felicity as she had someone to blame if she was late.

It was around this time that Felicity's mum decided to start a bed and breakfast for tourists to get the house properly furnished and a secondary-level boarding school was looming. Felicity was involved in the breakfast making and was warned to smile and say good morning to the guests when she was handing them their breakfast, a far cry from the face-like thunder that Felicity wore as she slammed their fry down in front of them. Poor father got himself a caravan so that he could still go around in his underwear. Mother slaved on but when a gentleman with a long beard and khaki shorts arrived she took one look at him and said she was full. How amazing he said as he had been assured in the hotel that she had spare rooms. It was the overflow from the hotel that she was dependent on. She heard subsequently that her bearded friend was a professor from Cork University. One night Angela and Felicity went off to the pier with two Northern Ireland boys who were staying in the hotel. They were cosy on the pier when suddenly the door of the car was yanked open by Mrs Walsh, Angela's mother, and the two girls were pulled out and walloped up the road home. Felicity was terrified that Mrs Walsh would tell her mother but not a word was said. Mrs Walsh had many loyal employees in the hotel who were only too glad to report any transgressions made by the children. This extended into the teens when rules were being tested, alcohol was forbidden but tested as an experiment furtively drunk out of lemonade bottles. Relationships were formed but rarely reached any advanced stages as the population was a changing scene with tourists coming and going. Mrs Walsh's oldest son went on to the priesthood and many of the staff would give her money to give him to say masses. He left the priesthood eventually and Mrs Walsh did not know what to say when they presented her with more money for masses so she told them that he had been layalised and could not say mass any more but the message that got out was that he was circumcised and couldn't say mass any more.

Felicity's mother and father took two weeks holiday every summer and Felicity could not believe her luck when her parents said she could stay with her friend Angela instead of going on the holiday. Unfortunately someone told her parents how little supervision there was of the young people in the hotel and she was forced in the end to go on holiday with them, a holiday no one enjoyed as Felicity refused to speak for the two weeks, ignored all beautiful views and was the epitome of a sullen spoilt child. One of the famous four parents separated and their daughter would write to Felicity and tell her not to tell daddy where she was living, leaving Felicity in no doubt that the father was the big bad wolf. This whole episode disturbed Felicity who started listening to her parents to see if there was any sign of them separating. After hearing a repeated argument on Sundays about dad not changing his clothes, or dressing smartly enough she decided it was only a matter of time before the same fate happened to her. She confided in her Uncle Brendan. It caused great hilarity behind the scenes, only discovered by Felicity in later life while reminiscing with her uncle Brendan on his deathbed. On asking her who she would go with she thought for a while and decided she would stay with whoever remained in the house, a very clever answer, designed to ruffle no feathers.

There was no secondary school locally and boarding school was the solution. Luckily her mother was friendly with a neighbour across the road who was from Dublin and she advised her on various boarding schools in Dublin, but because her mother left it so late she was forced to book one of the posh schools as the cram schools she favoured were full. As a result, Felicity ended up in Dominican Convent, Cabra, the mother house of the Dominican sisters so Felicity found herself in a school that specialised in producing young ladies but was not overly interested in academia. Here they taught among other things, ballroom dancing, elocution, deportment and how to be a young lady. Felicity was careful to hide her maths copies when she came home as the standard was so low but her mother guessed and she was not impressed and booked one of the cram schools for the following year. Felicity however had other ideas and announced she would run away if forced to go there. Mother was afraid and relented, the first battle was won. The boarding school was situated on the northside of Dublin in Cabra and had a primary-level boarding school, plus a school for the deaf. Many of the older deaf girls who had been abandoned worked in the convent as domestic staff and Cabra was their home. Later in life, Felicity was walking down O Connell St. with her boyfriend when three of these women who were standing outside Clearys recognised Felicity and rushed out to greet her making a racket and frightening the life out of the boyfriend who did not know what was happening. They were so lovely and friendly and were always kind to the girls in the school. Felicity who knew that she wanted to do medicine from an early age and that Latin was a requirement that she hated with a passion but there was no way out. After getting the bare forty per cent in the intermediate the nun known as the Fly who taught Latin told her to give it up and was none too pleased when she would not. She gave Felicity a hard time for two years ridiculing her ambition to go to college and do medicine, but Felicity struggled on and again got the bare forty per cent in the leaving cert, but it was a pass. Felicity also persuaded her parents to get a physics teacher in to give private grinds to herself and a friend of hers who was going to do science in university, and she helped with chemistry as well. The school was situated on landscaped grounds and was a very beautiful old building with a famous church attached, a place of silence and great reverence, a delightful place to chill out rather like modern pilates or yoga. Felicity during her stay there was getting a rare chance to go out to an opera but was stopped because she dared to go out through the church without putting on her hat. This was one time that beauty and reverence was cursed from on high. One of Felicity's friends got a car in her leaving cert year and drove into the school but unfortunately hit a nun and put her over the wall but luckily, she was not seriously injured, getting away with a dislocated shoulder. On another occasion, her father was driving her back to school and started stopping at pubs along the way to get a drink of brandy as he had a pain in his chest. When they reached Dublin, he went to his brother's G.P who admitted him straight away to Jervis Street Hospital as a coronary. He was only forty-seven years of age at that stage and it was the first of many coronaries treated conservatively as there was no stenting then.

Boarding school was uneventful, and Felicity made 3 very good friends that lasted a lifetime. Parents did not visit from one term to the next and expectations were low. The main highlight of her years there was when Tony O Reilly visited with his bride on their wedding day. His bride had an Aunt, a nun in the school. Her magnificent silver wedding dress was a thing of beauty never to be forgotten. The nuns would show a movie on a Sunday night and on one occasion there was a clip on famous art pieces which included, horror of horrors, nude pictures causing a dash by the nuns to cover the projector, an event which caused much clapping of hands by the students. She made a lasting friendship with a girl from Athboy called Antoinette Noonan. Her mother kept deep-litter hens and her father was a solicitor. She was often invited down for weekends and loved the big family effect, helping Mrs Noonan to gather the eggs and feed the hens. She was in awe of this woman who could be out attending the chickens and ten minutes later appear in her fur coat to accompany her husband out socially as he was president of the law society and did a lot of entertaining. They had five girls in the family so there was great company and comradery in that house over the weekend and he loved to pontificate, as all solicitors do, about the state of the world and implanting many deep thoughts in the mind to mull over for the next few weeks. It was the nearest thing to politics that Felicity got to in her teens. The Noonans loved classical music and played it right through Sunday lunch and gave Felicity a lasting love of classical music. One problem in that house was that there was no lock on the bathroom door and the father opened it by mistake one day while Felicity was in there. He shouted into her that he hoped he had not put her off her shot and always called her Sabastian as he could not remember Felicity. He often called to the school if he was in town and brought them out for a meal. Felicity remembers the first time it was to the Royal

Marine Hotel and Antoinette ordered a rare steak so Felicity ordered the same not having a clue what it was. How horrified was she when she saw the bloody offering that came out. The father knew well by her face and said he would get it better cooked but she said no it was grand and then had to cover every bite with a potato or a bit of mushroom to be able to swallow it. She eventually ended up loving a rare steak after her baptism of fire. Coming up to exam time some of the girls had torches and could study in bed and the pals would get into the bed to avail of the light. Rumours got out that some of the girls were getting into each other's beds and they were all called to the assembly room where a very red-faced nun tried to explain how it was dangerous and wrong to get into bed with another girl. Everyone was mystified and they sought advice from a girl from Westport who was much wiser about the ways of the world than them. She duly said that it was indeed dangerous and that you could get pregnant so that put an end to the studying in each other's beds. Mother superior informed Felicity's mother that they thought Felicity might become a nun, but mother knew her daughter too well and was in no way concerned nor did she seem anyway pleased that there might even be a vague chance of this happening.

It was during her time in boarding school that Felicity got the dreaded Asian flu and landed in the hospital where they were concerned about her heart murmur and the school were none too pleased that they had not been informed about it from her mother when Felicity came to the school. Her mother's overriding instructions were that there was to be no surgical intervention and the consultant Professor Abrahamson assured the mother that Felicity should lead a normal life and should survive to at least sixty all going well. There was quite a build-up of denial, secrecy and a psychological repression of Felicity being anything but perfect by her mother which rubbed off to a much lesser extent on Felicity. Luckily it had never interfered with her life so far or prevented her taking part in any activities. Felicity's case in the hospital which was a case of congenital heart disease was of great interest to the students but after having her chest examined by several students she burst into tears as she was mortified with the exposure at which point the consultant ordered everyone to leave her in peace. It may have set the seeds of her interest in medicine as a career, a rather dramatic way of dealing with the psychological trauma of secrecy surrounding her disability.

The next battle was careers for Felicity who knew from the age of seven that she wanted to become a doctor and came up from the beach to announce it much to her mother's alarm in case anyone would hear her coming out with this nonsense, "you are losing the run of yourself", was her response. The dreaded leaving cert loomed but was not so bad as you got into medicine with a pass leaving cert if you had Latin. You could buy the Matrick and the only other problem was the fees if parents could afford it. "A nice teaching job said mother", "no" said Felicity, medicine is what I want and so the battle began. Mother headed up to U. C. D, got the syllabus for science and even got some of the books. The next move was to invite one of the friends from school, Antoinette, for a holiday, as this girl was going to study science in U. C. D. and mother thought she might persuade Felicity to do likewise but to no avail. Two days before going to register at UCD, Felicity went out to her dad who was fixing a puncture on the Morris minor car and said dad I want to do medicine, not science "and who will pay for you if anything happens me?" He already had one heart attack, "my mother, she is working, she can pay". "Ok. If that is what you want". Felicity skipped into the kitchen to tell her mum that daddy says I can do medicine. Mother's reply was you will never be fit for it, the greatest incentive she could have given to Felicity who from that day on was determined to prove her mother wrong. The system in medical school was to admit about 300 to pre-med and at the end of the year, only 120 would get through. A very fair system but also a very expensive one for parents whose children did not get through as they were out the year's fees with nothing to show for it.

CHAPTER THREE UNIVERSITY

University was a whole new ball game. The whole experience was challenging but endlessly interesting and varied. Students usually stayed in halls run by nuns and there was an 11 pm curfew. Here lifelong friendships were made. Felicity was put in with the science students thanks to mother but it didn't really cause a problem but rather a widening of experiences. Mother felt that if Felicity stayed in a hall of residency run by the nuns, she would be safer and would have to be in every night unless she got a pass. She was duly booked into Dominican Hall in Stephens Green. It was a fact of life that going from boarding school in Dublin to university was not the wrench that a first away from home would be and for Felicity, it held no separation or loneliness and was in fact a natural progression from school to college. It is something that is not prorated about boarding schools and how they make the transition seamless. Coming from a strict boarding school to halls of residence run by the same nuns was so exciting. In Cabra the nuns couldn't talk after ten o'clock so when Felicity and her friend Antoinette were allowed in the final year in Cabra to attend the Tostal and stay in Dominican Hall they were thrilled but decided to give the Tostal a skip and go to a movie instead. As they returned after ten o'clock they were happy that no one could question them but to their horror, the nun who opened the door wanted to know all about the Tostal. Felicity had no doubt that she knew well they had not been near the Tostal after their pathetic attempt to cover their tracks as they stuttered and bluffed their way through her interrogation. College was teaming with students, lectures were held daily, and the explosive wave of medical knowledge that was going to define you as a doctor felt really overwhelming. The gradual assumption of medical power was welcomed and stored. Even at this early stage, Felicity felt she was so privileged to be part of this universe. Looking around at all these big confident men who had come down from the 6 counties all with A levels in physics and chemistry, Felicity thought maybe her mother had been right but spurred on by her mother's words and her own ambition she soldiered on but also enjoyed campus life. Hops in Newman House, the Irrawaddy's Hop, The Crystal in Camden Street and running to the hall in bare feet to make the curfew of midnight. The posh schools came into their own at university level as their students were accomplished in abstracting the relevant knowledge from large textbooks, a skill not acquired by the cram schools who were used to reams of notes. And were mystified when presented with large textbooks. Felicity was used to studying in libraries and quickly assessed a quiet library in St Vincent's hospital just beside the Dominican hall where she was staying. There was a large garden attached to Newman House which was part of the college. A second Med student approached Felicity to enquire if she had her plot in the garden for botany which she would need. He was selling his at a knockdown price of five pounds so Felicity and her money were parted and her helpful friend had a good story for the pub, but never again, once bitten twice shy. It was a time of political unrest in Ireland and the I.R.A was actively recruiting and had modest success in the college. If you were being educated by the British army you had to sing dumb as it was quite dangerous. Felicity's parents were alarmed when she arrived home with a United Irishman's paper. She had some empathy with the cause having heard tales of the atrocities of the black and tans in her grannies as a child, luckily she was too busy studying and living to get involved. The medics were not recruited as actively as other faculties probably because they had full days every day. It is a time of life when students are looking for a cause to establish their own identity and like the call of religion there are other less savoury pursuits actively recruited.

In the class, inevitably, there was a mixture of all sides and nationalities, Indian, Malaysian, Chinese and African to mention a few but over 80 per cent were Irish. Seating was arranged alphabetically, so Felicity was up with the Os. Her friend beside her was a T. O Brien and he was from a farm down the country. The lecturer called him down one day to tell him she had a special interest in him and would help him in any way she could. She would be monitoring his progress. It transpired that she had mixed him up with another D. O Brian who was a consultant's son and the parents were personal friends of hers so T. O Brien got dropped like a hot potato. There was another student who carried one of those old small brown cases who would drop everything if the angelus bell rang and do his praying no matter where he was. He was a solitary figure in the class who took 14 years to qualify so eventually they had to let him through. University hall where Felicity stayed was on St Stephen's green and due to the number of students it was not easy to get the bathroom free when you wanted it but they were next door to the Shelbourne Hotel and Felicity and her friends would sneak over to the Shelbourne to enjoy a bit of luxury including free shampoo. It was a time when bedrooms were not on suite and there were many bathrooms in the corridors. Eventually, they were caught and duly barred but it had taken a long time to catch them. Money was scarce and jobs were not gettable as the unemployment was sky high. This left students very strapped for money. Student jobs were few and far between and medical school was expensive. It was still a time when it was frowned upon for a female to go into a bar alone or branch out on her own to work. As it was the 60s the liberal tide was flowing. Skirts were short. Tampax had hit the market and there were various rumours that if you used them you had to confess it in confession and really it was doubtful if you were a virgin after their use. This did not surprise Felicity as after her first battle with the Tampax she had to cycle out to a grind in Crumlin given by one of the laboratory assistants, necessary to pass your practical laboratory exam. The same laboratory assistant who was responsible for setting up the experiments with the frogs had all expired by the time the class came, and he was frantically trying to revive them by throwing adrenaline on them.

Exams came and went, and Felicity struggled on, failing an exam here and there, but never had to repeat a year. Going into the dissecting room where the dead bodies known as stiffs are is a daunting experience for some students. Normally you are assigned to a male or female stiff and there are up to 7 students working on the one stiff. You are encouraged to compare the male with the female. Felicity was on a female stiff and when she got as far as the abdomen in the dissection she found the ovaries so off she went to compare with the male but she could not find any testicles in the male abdomen and nobody seemed to know why, even the demonstrators walked away when she asked them. Eventually one of her friends said "you have no wee brothers" they are not there at all, they are down below in the male".

You were warned to treat the stiffs with respect and not to forget that they were once hard-working human beings who were unselfish enough to donate their bodies to science. Felicity would cringe when someone would tell her that they were going to donate their bodies to research as she felt that respect went out the door very soon after you got familiar with your stiff. It would be interesting to do a survey on how many doctors donate their bodies to science. It was a time of falling in love and Felicity had her share of crushes but from a distance. One of her pals was determined to advance one of these lovesick desires and manipulated Felicity to be near the object of her dreams in the dance hall where she gave Felicity a big push so she stumbled into him whereupon he turned and asked her friend to dance. Socialising mainly consisted of hops in the clubs, going to the movies, frequenting the local pubs after studying in the library all evening, and attending the debating society like the L and H society famously attended by people like Joyce and Yeats in their day. Thumbing lifts was rife and going off down to Glendalough, Bray, and Dalkey were normal weekend past times. Going home was not on the agenda as no one could afford it. Many of the students came from the boarding school ethos, it did not enter their heads to go home at weekends, unlike the present time when trains are bursting at the seams on a Friday evening. Of course, home means clean clothes, stocking up on food and some tender loving care over the weekend.

About 3rd year in medical school you start to get into real medicine in that you got working on the wards with real patients and it is at this stage that the class splits to go to either the Mater Hospital or St Vincents to continue training. Felicity loved the Mater and travelled across town each day. You are assigned to a consultant and Felicity worked with Dr Alton. He drove a Silver Cloud Rolls Royce and would bring his students and staff out one night a year. The night that he invited the team that Felicity belonged to, it was to the Stephens Green Club and he sent a message that he would be late but to go ahead to the bar and order whatever they wanted and he would meet them there. He was late by half an hour and the boys made full use of the time to become seven sheets to the wind by the time he arrived, so a great night was had by all. He left Felicity home to her flat, in Appian Way, but it was 2am and she was bitterly disappointed that none of her friends saw her getting out of the silver cloud. She had many adventures in the Mater, losing her stethoscope and putting up a notice to return it to her drawers if found or when sent to take blood from a patient in room 5. She went to room 5 armed with a needle and syringe. She was a little surprised to find the patient fully dressed but as he was a private patient she didn't pay much heed. She had completed the task when the real patient walked out of the toilet and it transpired that she had taken a visitor's blood who had sat there and done as he was told. One night in casualty a patient who had passed out due to an excess dose of insulin was brought in by his wife but was quickly cured after getting an injection of glucose into his system and was ready for discharge. His wife and her friend who was with her and who turned out to be a politician and a doctor wanted him admitted as the wife was helping him with his canvassing for an election which was imminent. The politician was ultra-friendly and wondered where he had met Felicity before and how grateful he would be if she would admit the patient. When this did not work he got quite eloquent about the dangers of diabetes and finally, he got irate and demanded that she ring a higher authority which she did, the registrar, and explained the case but he also refused admission. I doubt she would fight the system so adamantly today. On another occasion on hospital rounds, the consultant asked a student to look in the male patient's mouth and report what he saw whereupon the student proudly proclaimed that he could see the vulva. You will make medical history so said the consultant. This student was always impeccably dressed even wearing a waistcoat and was often mistaken by the patients as the consultant so he was brought down to earth with a bang. Felicity doing casualty one night had a small fat man in his 50s come in complaining of being raped by two prostitutes. She duly put him in a room with a glass window and kept looking in at him every 2 to 3 hours to see if he had gone home, which he did after ten hours. She had no idea what to do with him as there were only protocols for female rape, not males.

Every day was full of action and one day was more interesting than the other. There were also rotations through gynaecology and obstetrics. Here a male patient being investigated for infertility was told to bring in a sample of semen to get a sperm count done. He came with a large jar full of what was obviously urine to the amusement of the students who were severely reprimanded by the consultant for embarrassing the poor man by laughing. This consultant always seemed to have a finger ready to examine his patients. If any woman had a heavy coat or several layers of clothing he would just pop her on the bed and examine the position of the baby through her clothes.

Felicity's best friend gave one of the patients a massive overdose of insulin and had to sit beside the patient for twenty-four hours and run in a glucose solution whenever he started to go unconscious, Felicity helped her over the twenty-four hours so that she could go to the toilet and eat something. Another time a prominent politician arrived at the Mater Private following a road traffic accident and suffering from a deep vein thrombosis. Instead of allowing the nurses to give him his drugs the intern was requested to give them. As the vials used in the private hospital were a different strength from those used in the public hospital, he got an overdose of heparin to prevent clotting and the consultant had to be informed. The patient was given vitamin k to counteract it and Felicity who was the junior doctor got a severe dose of fury from the consultant. After a very busy night on duty with no sleep and on again the next day Felicity was verbally attacked by one of Dr Altons patients for talking to another doctor, ignoring him and being rude in the extreme so she told him to clear off home which he did and then waited in fear and trembling for Dr Alton to tell him what had happened but he supported her fully.

It was common to have to resort to grinds where lectures left a lot to be desired. This was especially true with the practical side of medicine like dissecting frogs and dogfish and other laboratory work. In physiology, the lecturer who was mediocre gave a great grind at the end of the year which was necessary to take to get the exam so off everyone trotted to his house for the grinds given over four weeks before the exam.
On the wards, the nuns ruled with an iron fist and God help you if you got blood on the sheets when you were taking blood samples. They were sticklers for time and would even criticise your dress if they thought it was not appropriate. They ran an impressive system in the wards and they were meticulously clean. Felicity's first attempt at taking a blood sample was a disaster as she pulled the plunger out the top of the

syringe and of course all the blood spilt. Another patient was in a rush to go to the loo, a number two but was not allowed out of bed and as Felicity felt sorry for him she managed to get the commode up on the bed for him to use. Unfortunately, ward rounds happened to arrive and everyone was convulsed with laughter except Sr. Cathriona who was the nun in charge.

Exams were hard and Felicity had to study hard, but she got first-class honours in paediatrics. On the day of the exam, she got a child of 3 to examine who was suffering from hypothyroidism and his development was delayed. The examiners kept asking what else she had found but she was blank so eventually, they said what about his walk, oh he can walk, really, please demonstrate. Felicity got out her bar of chocolate said a quick prayer and held out the bar and the child walked to get it. That was the first time he walked and thence she got her honours.
D-day came and the final Med was attacked and completed. Felicity's Aunty Rose was given the task of getting the results when they were put up on the board in U.C.D. and there she saw Felicity's name but went back 3 times to check it out. When she rang Felicity's mum to tell her the name was on the board "are you sure" said her mum, "I am sure" "are you sure that you are sure". Poor mother could not believe her ears.
After final Med exams, Felicity was completely bunched and her only thought was sleep. Felicity and her four pals headed to Achill Island, the far-flung reaches of the earth as far as they were concerned and booked into a B and B where for three days they only surfaced for breakfast and back to bed, cancelled all cleaning and checking of rooms and they were a complete mystery to the nosey landlady who could not figure out these 4 four young people who were essentially recluse since arrival.

Getting an internship in your chosen hospital is difficult but the males the previous year had disgraced themselves in the residency and this year the authorities were partial to taking on females, so Felicity got an internship in her Alma Mater for one year. Felicity was working in the liver ward and had a room in the residency. The residency is where the junior doctors live and where a great social life flourishes. It also provides ready-made company as the doctors who are off-duty socialise

together. Felicity will tell of going to Howth on a sunny Sunday and driving the car on the pavement passing all the cars to get there.
You worked long 12-hour shifts and no one complained as 60 to 70 hours a week was common, you had a senior house officer, a registrar and a consultant above you able to offer help and advice. A stint of 6 months on the surgical side and 6 months on the medical side completed the internship.

On the surgical side Felicity worked for the Genito urinary surgeon who was none too happy when he saw her as she was just the bare five foot and as he said looked like a child. He was a popular surgeon with the clergy and hoy poly of Dublin and wondered how they would accept this doctor who would have to do bladder washouts after prostate surgery to avoid blockage and he let his annoyance be known but by the time Felicity had done her 6 months he maintained that you could not judge the book by the cover and that she was a little trooper.
The consultant fancied himself as a Gaelic speaker and proceeded to talk in Irish but Felicity who was a native Irish speaker from Donegal was quick to put him in his box as he only had pigeon Irish.
Felicity at this time got good news from her mother, she had won 100 pounds in the prize bonds. This Felicity proceeded to spend on a massive party to mothers horror who thought her daughter had lost the plot. It probably was a lot of money to squander as this was 1969 and somewhat out of character for Felicity.

When Felicity was in her final medical year in college many of the students were going to America to work in hospitals for the summer. Once again Felicity's mother put down her foot and said no but she was generous with the pocket money and Felicity was over 21 so she saved hard to get the fifty pounds for the ticket and succeeded. The parents came to see her off at the airport, but mother asked no questions about the hospital she was going to which was in Milwaukee. They offered her forty pounds, but she said she did not need it. She produced a cigarette and smoked it just to copper fasten her independence. It was a big deal at that time to go to America. That magical place where the parcels of clothes used to come from to clothe the family relatives back home where else but Uncle Sam.

The plane was full of rowdy medical students aided on by alcohol carrying them across the Atlantic to hit New York. At that time you could get a 99-dollar ticket for the greyhound buses which allowed you to travel for 99 days all over America. It even provided an overnight as a lot of the trips were done at night so no need for accommodation.
On reaching New York everyone scattered to their various destinations pre-arranged and booked for three months. As Felicity was going to Milwaukee, she had company as far as Chicago and was then on her own. It was the one time in her life that she took a sleeping tablet to get some sleep between New York and Chicago, but it knocked her out and frightened her so much that she never touched sleeping tablets again. She arrived at the hospital at 3 am but no one knew of her arrival or what the story was so they put her in the bishop's room until the next day when she could be sorted. She was given a room in the residence where there were 14 other junior doctors all from the Philippines, half male and half female. They took her under their wing and were incredibly good to her, including her in all their social activities and weekend picnics. Felicity will never forget their kindness. As they could cook in the residence Felicity also became a good Filipino cook.

One of the first things Felicity did was to write home as there were no phones that time, unfortunately she posted the letter in a bin thinking it was a post box. Meanwhile back in Ireland, the parents were going frantic as they had not even gotten the name of the hospital. They even went as far as contacting Interpol. Felicity was subsequently told that her mother almost had a nervous breakdown. Felicity made good friends with one of the nurses called Mary Marcinac who invited her to her house and wised her up on all the workings of the hospital. One of the consultants, a big fat Italian invited her to his house for dinner, but her friend warned her not to go as he was single and had a reputation with the ladies and was partial to a bit of hanky panky. This image of a consultant was far removed from the awe they were held in Ireland. Even though Felicity was only a medical student she was given much more responsibility than back in Ireland and the experience was wonderful. The hospital was built beside lake Michigan and there was a beach there called doctors beach where they went swimming, play ball, and have barbecues. The Filipinos were very modest, and the different sexes would separate at the beach to get togged out, an occurrence that seemingly only pertained to daylight.

The time in America was so enjoyable and Felicity was able to visit her two Uncles, one in New Jersey called Kevin who was sound and one in Winchester called Vincent near Washington. Her visit to Vincent got off to a bad start. She was the only passenger in the bus for the last 50 miles of the journey and had got chatting with the bus driver about fishing as he fished the rivers and the lakes and Felicity was a deep sea fisherwoman and they exchanged many stories of their various escapades so when they reached Winchester he asked her to have a cup of coffee while they were waiting for her uncle to come. When he came, all 6 feet of him, he was not enamoured to find her up at the bar having a coffee with a man and read the riot act all the way back to the house about not talking to strange men in America. It was quite an introduction to someone she had never met before.

Felicity had got two of the current popular records for his two boys aged seven and eleven but when he saw them, he said I would not let my boys play those. I will put them in the attic. He then started to do a barbecue in the garden and Felicity seeing the lovely weather changed into her swimsuit. She noticed the flames coming from the barbecue and told the uncle he needed to be careful not to burn the steaks whereupon he said do you want to do them yourself. It appeared that Felicity could do nothing right or maybe it was the bathing suit that was annoying him as he had neighbours on both sides.
He had said that he would show her Washington but after two days and no sign of a trip, Felicity arrived down the stairs to announce that she was going to Washington. But I can't go today, says Vincent, no problem says Felicity I am going on my own and off she went. What she never told him was that she was followed by a big 6-foot man, so she had to stay where there were loads of people. Each morning Vincent went to mass and Felicity decided to join him. Where are you going, to mass with you, no way you could ever keep up with me walking, he wore size 11 shoes, it was definitely time to go back to Milwaukee. The Uncles subsequent report on the visit was that she was headstrong and difficult and despite invites during his visits to Ireland he never came to visit or

even answered them. He was a good-looking six-footer who ruled his household with a rod of iron, however he had a sad life, his first wife dying in childbirth after being told never to get pregnant as this might happen. The wife's family turned against him subsequently and would not allow him to come to the funeral. He married secondly to a lady, an only child who was a complete hypochondriac and spent most of her time in bed. On Felicity's visit, she only saw her once coming to the kitchen so one had to forgive him for his aggressive manner.

It was the time of the riots in America in 1967 and they were particularly bad in Chicago which was on the route to Milwaukee, they were also bad in Milwaukee itself. Felicity would talk about waiting at a bus stop and she could see the fighting a quarter of a mile down the road. Some of her Irish friends came up to visit her at the weekends from Ohio but could only get as far as Chicago due to the riots, they were put up in a hotel there. Very many people came to the emergency room in the hospital during these troubled times and many of them needed stitches for slash wounds. In this way, Felicity got great experience but when it came to taking out the stitches it was so difficult as the stitches were the same colour as their skin, black and so hard to see.

Felicity did some travelling. She went to visit her friends in the Mayo Clinic in Rochester Minnesota not realising that one day she would be back here as a patient. She visited Expo1967 in Montreal and spent some time in New York and New Jersey. The whole trip was a wonderful experience with a steep learning curve but she missed her parents, the boat at home and her friends. It was her first taste of being on her own and far from home. The hospital was varied and interesting and you were given much more responsibility than in Ireland, often being on your own on night duty.

Once back on the Emerald Isle Felicity got her driving licence she used to drive all makes of cars as the pals often went to a small bar out in the Muckish mountains after the hotel shut down for the night and she was not drinking therefore the ideal chauffeur. No matter what time she came in she would be up early the next morning to help her mother with the Bed and Breakfast

Around this time Felicity reached the magic age of twenty-one but there was no attempt to have a celebration of any kind. A friend's mother baked her a cake and the friends had it that evening. Felicity set about organising a party at a later date in her house to be held after the hotel dance finished but no matter how much she begged mother to allow alcohol, even cider, the answer was no so it was just food consumed on the sitting room floor with music. It was as if mother could not bear to see her daughter growing up.

On one of her visits home, she brought a Scottish friend who was a psychiatrist from the hospital called Stephen to show him some of the sights of Donegal. One famous Sunday she brought him to Derry. As they were driving over the Foyle river all was peaceful and serene. On arrival, Felicity thought to show him the Bog side, a famous republican area of Derry. They were walking up the Bog side when Stephen said why are all these soldiers lying in the gardens with their guns cocked. Felicity had not been paying any heed and only then noticed the soldiers lying in the gardens of the houses with guns raised and all the people at the upstairs window looking out. There was no one, only them walking on the road and she knew immediately that something was very wrong. She warned Stephen not to talk with his pronounced British accent and she was afraid to turn back as she feared they would be shot.

She decided to try to get to the City hotel and find out what was going on, they proceeded to the diamond square and down Shipset street and met all these soldiers in combat gear and with gas masks. There were also men being held up against walls with a gun to their backs. Priests were here and there running around trying to help the wounded. When they got to the hotel it was mobbed with reporters. Felicity went over to the telephones to hear what was being said and learned that there had been many shootings that day with heavy casualties.

The whole thing was terrifying, and they still had to get back to the car to get home. Felicity had told Stephen to say they were visiting Altnagalvin hospital if stopped but on the way out they were questioned separately and Felicity realised she did not know where Altnagalvin was and said

the centre of Derry but because their stories differed they were brought to headquarters for questioning but eventually convinced the authorities that they were innocent mostly due to Stephen who had good identification with him. On going home at the border they came across a bad accident with bodies all over the road, Being the first on the scene they had to get out to help and Felicity thought they would be shot as soon as they got out of the car but that did not happen, and it was only minutes before the ambulance came. Felicity warned Stephen not to tell the parents that they were in Derry although Felicity's white slacks were spattered with blood at this stage from helping the crash victims.
When they arrived home mother exclaimed that she was all day worrying that they might have gone to Derry as there was a terrible shooting there that day. This was the day that became known as Bloody Sunday in Derry and made headlines all over the world.

At some stage, she met a nice lad who worked in Trinity in the science laboratory and had a sailing boat in Sutton. Life was magical for a time and she brought him home but made out he had given her a lift home as he was visiting his brother who lived nearby. After his constant re-appearance over the next few days the penny dropped but he in no way measured up to her mother's expectations and she even went as far as to say that he might be a little retarded in her next letter.
Unfortunately, the spark was not there, and they parted after a year. Felicity would say that the sailing boat was the main attraction and she caused quite a stir one day when she came into the Mater dining room in her shorts.

The day the internship in America came to an end was described by Felicity as one of the saddest days of her life. Medical life only begins in earnest after the internship, you must decide what you want to specialise in. Felicity thought maybe child psychiatry and duly got a job in the Crichton Royal Hospital in Dumfries in Scotland in the child psychiatry unit with a consultant called Dr Rogers.

CHAPTER 4 TRAINING
*********************************/

There were over thirty-five children in the paediatric residential care unit ranging in age from six to fourteen. Looked after by a very dedicated and loving staff. Regularly one of the children would run away and you could spend all day trawling the country looking for them with the aid of the police. Part of your work involved visiting their homes, talking to their parents These children were in patients, but they all came from broken homes of one type or another, alcoholic parents, jailbirds, violent parents, sexual abuse at home, and the list goes on. The children are not the problems the parents are. Felicity had to get them to talk about their problems which she was good at but where did it get you? She spent her time playing snakes and ladders and wondering why she spent 7 years in college, so after 6 months she changed to adult psychiatry and found that even worse as a cure was rarely obtained.

Felicity at that stage believed in God and was Catholic, she used to bring the catholic children to mass on a Sunday from the residential home and of course they got a treat after mass like ice cream or sweets which they really enjoyed. It took this experience to teach her that she was the type of doctor who liked to see results like a sore throat that you would treat, and it would get better. Apart from career-wise life was good on the social front in Scotland. She made some long-lasting friends including a Belfast girl called Doreen. They moved out of the residence to a rented cottage called Kelton Lodge. There they acquired Mattie the dog to add to the Volkswagen which her father had given her complete with the holes in the floor due to being stationed by the sea and which Felicity filled with cement known after as the cement beetle where it competed with Rosie the red triumph belonging to Doreen. Mattie was useful to bring along to the pub in the evening and if they saw a good-looking guy at the bar they would encourage Mattie to go over near him and then rush over to apologise on Mattie's behalf. The problem was that you had to find a pub that allowed dogs in and then you had to find a good-looking man preferably alone.

The lodge was on the banks of the Nithe River and they asked a third girl called Naomi to share with them. They were both occupational therapists and the mix was perfect.

There was a scarcity of females in Dumfries as it was an industrial town and a social club in the hospital ensured them a social life. Felicity felt it was one of the best years of her life. She and her pals joined classes in advanced driving as this they reckoned would have a good selection of young males. They were out driving on the ice and skidding all over the place. They got their certificates out of it but no male companion however they got a reduction in their car insurance.

The only way home was by boat from Stranraer to Larne, it was quite a distance, so she rarely went. Doreen was from Belfast and this was much more accessible than Donegal, so she often went home with Doreen at weekends. The hospital had a heated swimming pool and staff had a key so there were great swimming competitions among the friends. The whole set-up lent itself to singing songs, games and comradery, so life was good.

She made friends with a medical colleague working with her who had a sailing boat and Felicity was in her element to be back on the water. One evening her friend did not turn up and Felicity went off looking for her only to discover that she had committed suicide the night before. It upset Felicity greatly as she had no inkling that there was any problem and felt inadequate and guilty over it as a doctor and a friend.
The bluer side of life quickly became apparent to Felicity in adult Psychiatry and any bit of innocence that might have survived medical school was quickly dispelled. She found it a sad tedious speciality with often no light at the end of the tunnel. There was none of the obvious relief of pain and suffering that occurred with treatment in other specialities. At least she had established that she needed to see reward for her work and that it would take a better person than her to continue in this speciality.

It was the first time she had her own money and time to enjoy it. She bought her mother a new electric cooker as up to now she cooked on a gas cooker. It was delivered and sat for many long years in the garage. It was a case of I know better than you what to cook on, no communication was entered into before it was bought.

As it was nearing the end of her stint in Scotland Felicity became more focused on her career and resolved to specialise in children's health. She applied for a paediatric job in Galway under professor Mc Nicholas who was a great paediatrician and also a friendly man. As the team wanted some outside blood, she got the job despite opposition from the local scene which she only heard about much later. As she was now a senior house officer, she had an intern working under her, but this doctor had been there a few months already. On her first night, she was called at 3 am to a two and a half-year-old who would not stop crying. Felicity examined the child thoroughly but could find no great problem or evidence of illness but the intern urged her that the child was really sick and she should get the professor in, so against her better judgement she sent for the professor. He stood for a full five minutes observing the child, requested a rubber glove and diagnosed constipation leaving Felicity red-faced with embarrassment. Galway was a lovely city small enough to make you familiar with the ins and outs of it all. The colleagues were friendly and competitive. Exams loomed large on the agenda which involved the Diploma in Child Health, It was a shared learning effort with barely time to eat coming up to the exam.

It was around this time that Felicity began to feel unwell. She lost her appetite and lost weight going down to 7 stone. Rather than complain she struggled on with a gruelling schedule for about six weeks but was well aware that all was not right and then eventually she needed help so rather than admit to her colleagues or any consultant she knew she took herself off to a consultant in the Richmond hospital in Dublin who did not know her. The waiting room was full and Felicity was last in. She was well aware of how tired he would be at this stage of the day and also as she looked OK she was afraid he would slot her into the worried well brigade who were classed as the greatest time wasters going. He was puzzled by her symptoms but assured her that he believed her and that it needed sorting in the hospital which he would arrange the next day. He made a joke as she left that he hoped he was driving in a different direction as he did not want to meet her. She sat her diploma in child health just before going to the hospital and a colleague who was behind her at the exam said she had several rigours during the exam. She was really worried about her.

She was admitted to the hospital the next day and was put down as suffering from apraxia of unknown origin which was extensively investigated initially without any diagnosis but eventually after calling in a cardiologist Dr Blake from the Mater Hospital her old Alma Mater he diagnosed it as subacute bacterial endocarditis a condition that then carried a thirty per cent mortality rate and was treated with intravenous antibiotics for six to eight weeks. It is basically an infection of the heart valve or valves usually in people who already have a cardiac condition such as congenital heart disease. Being on the other side of the fence was an enlightening experience for Felicity. She reassured the parents that it was only a slight infection which would take time to clear so they did not get unduly bothered. She was in a ward with four others and learned much about the perceptions of the laypeople regarding the doctors, nurses etc. never divulging that she was a medic. During her stay there the membership exams were held for those aspiring to become consultants. Felicity was asked would she mind being an exam patient as her case was rare and interesting, so she agreed.
She was passed over to a very nervous membership candidate who managed to knock over a huge drum of oxygen on entering the ward. When he was finished examining her and preparing his case he was amazed when suddenly the patient started to tell him all the relevant facts in case he was missing anything,

Felicity was on an antibiotic drip all this time and it was very difficult to get her veins so eventually only the anaesthetist could get them. One morning the nurses decided to change the giving set on the drip. It was a double giving set and Felicity was worried about the needle getting dislodged so she was not watching the giving set which they turned on without running it through and this meant that Felicity got over fifty ml of air into her vein. This caused her to collapse with an air embolism. When she woke up all the emergency team were around her no one knew what happened but Felicity knew straight away that she had got a large air embolism and was lucky to survive it. Maybe you could call it one of the nine lives. She said all's well that ends well.

Near her last days in the hospital, the consultant said he would let her out overnight to see how she got on. He was not to know that she had her car in the car park and off she headed for Galway. On reaching there she contacted her pals who said Professor Mc Nicholas was having a party that night and all his team were invited so off she went until two am to partake of anything going wine and all. Professor told a joke, his party piece about children who have a crooked penis, he reassures the parents that as long as the child can pee straight and fuck straight there is no problem. Felicity was quick to inform him that as soon as she joined his team she had heard he would tell that joke that it was his party piece to be met with stunned silence . . . The morning had her heading back to the hospital in Dublin to resume her perch in the ward. This episode stretched over the Christmas period and her parents came to visit. Her mother was fussing about meeting her sister and as it was their first visit in eight weeks Felicity felt emotional, lonely and a bit deserted and dissolved into tears which freaked them out as this was someone who never cried, keeping in mind that they had no idea of the seriousness of the illness, they found it hard to fathom. She was allowed out for dinner on a Christmas day trip and all attached. This was because she was a medic and hopefully could manage the drip if anything went wrong.

After discharge work resumed as normal but she had to make up the two months that she had missed. Her next placement was in Sligo General hospital in maternity under Dr Donovan a dedicated obstetrician where she would get first-hand knowledge of neonates and the miracle of giving birth and all its joys and sorrows. Again it was residency accommodation and hence ready-made friends and Felicity was delighted with the whole experience of a small hospital where there was cross-cover and wide experience to be got especially as there was an excellent paediatric unit presided over by Dr Mc Donagh who allowed her to join in on rounds and allowed her to do the blood exchanges on the rhesus negative babies These babies are born to mothers who are rhesus negative but who form antibodies to their babies blood if the babies are rhesus positive, this affects the babies when they are born. This no longer occurs as you can be vaccinated against it if you are a rhesus-negative mum. Felicity had decided at this stage that she wanted to specialise in children and become a paediatrician.

The residency in Sligo hospital was on the top floor of the new building and housed ten junior doctors. It had a lovely view out over the town taking in the majestic Benbulben. There was a fully equipped kitchen with gourmet cooking done especially by the foreign doctors and many parties were held. You had to keep your bedroom door locked as the young doctors if they came in late would take you out of the bed at any hour of the night and send you up and down in the lift three or four times. On the way up to the residency there were plants and flowers which were watered at night by the returning doctors.

As Sligo was not far from Donegal, she could go home more often. Her parents had built a new house and still had the old one, they had no problem with Felicity taking her pals up for weekends. The pals ran out of milk on one weekend and that posed no problem as one of the lads took to the fields to milk the first cow he saw. It was one of the weekends around Easter when she came back to Sligo that she met the gang heading out to Rosses Point. They persuaded her to tag along.

CHAPTER 5 ROMANCE
****

It was Easter Monday and Felicity was feeling very fed up as she had met a nice fellow the previous night in the hotel at home who wanted to meet again but she had decided to go back to Sligo and now regretted it. so arriving in the Yeats County hotel at a dance did not enamour her. Felicity was asked to dance by this fellow who had his coat on and then asked a second time, they hit it off and he offered to escort her home and although she had a lift with the pals she threw caution to the wind and accepted. This turned to dismay when she discovered that there were two other lads with him and it was not his own car but the dice was cast and he wanted to know where she lived. He did not blink an eye when she said the hospital and she was safely deposited with a date for the next week. She arranged to meet him in town and it was not until the fifth date that he discovered she was a doctor which he took in his stride. Initially she thought he had no car as they always travelled in her beetle having met in town but it transpired that his previous experience of girlfriends was that they judged him on the car he drove and fell in love with the car rather than him. He had just got a rather sassy triumph sports car and was slow to produce it but Felicity was immune to such possessions.

On one occasion late in the evening he had to go back home after getting an s.o.s that his cattle had broken out and Felicity went with him. He invited her in for a cup of tea and of course she said yes as she was keen to see where he lived. He lived with an elderly housekeeper and he was at pains to make no noise as she could be quite wicked He duly produced two cups but progress was stalled until he turned and asked her did she know how to make tea. Felicity found this amazing but as he said neither he nor his siblings were welcome in the kitchen as that was the housekeeper's domain and as they ran a big business including a pub, taxies an undertaking business and gravel pits plus a farm he never had to cook. He would tell the story of going to France with the boy scouts to camp and as jobs were shared he had to cook the potatoes. He put them in the pot, with no water or washing and put them on the fire. Of course, they were burned black. Felicity knew there was going to be a steep learning curve ahead if ever this romance went the full hog. Berks which was his pet name enjoyed similar things to Felicity and was a well-known rugby player in Sligo and Garbally College   It transpired that when Felicity meet him he was seeing another girl and two timed for a while but eventually the day came and he had to make a choice and the choice was Felicity.

Felicity had applied to the children's hospital in Toronto which was a super hospital to train as a paediatrician to further her ambition to become a child specialist. Around this time a work colleague sat her down and gave her a lecture about the nice boyfriend she had, his good name, his sporting feats etc. or did she want to become an old spinster living on her own. With all the good advice and her gra for Berks, she opted to forget paediatrics and go for general practice and see how things went. General practice requires some expertise in maternity, childcare and especially psychiatry which she had gotten in Scotland, so she was well qualified.

The romance was going from good to better and a lovely old rectory built in 1847 came on the market in Berks small village 20 miles from Sligo which he felt they should buy. Felicity who was from a conservative professional family who abhorred debt had great reservations about going into debt and they were not even engaged so after going to 9 thousand she wanted to pull out. However after opting out of a Friday, Berks sent her an SOS to meet him on the mail coach road and more persuasion went on until finally he got her to agree to a two thousand jump to put off other candidates and they secured the rectory at long last. Subsequently she heard that there was a local legend that it might be haunted and this put off a lot of the locals from bidding. Their main contender was a dentist from Belfast who was told he had the rectory of a Friday evening but on Monday that he had not got it. He being from Northern Ireland felt that it was tied up in catholic/protestant politics and pulled out. Luckily, he hadn't put down a deposit on Friday, so they were still in with a chance and it was finally bought for 12 thousand.
It was around this time just before they bought the rectory that Felicity brought Berks to Donegal and during the weekend they met one of

Felicity's friends an architect who proceeded to tell them that a dentist friend of hers from Belfast was interested in an old rectory in Ballymote which they had surveyed and that it was in good nick. Felicity hastened to tell her they were also interested in the same property but at that stage she had heard the good news about the structure and the survey prior to buying it. Berks sent Felicity to view the premises as he felt that it was better to have a female negotiating it but warned her to find out how many cattle it would feed. Felicity who had not a clue went to view the rectory and kept looking up at these high ceilings and asking how many cattle it would feed. At this stage, the estate agent had his arm around her telling her not to worry about cattle. He had no idea where she came from and wanted to know if she was married as he had a nice little man in mind for her. Felicity noticed a lot of dots on the back of the shutters in the sitting room and thought it was woodworm, but it was where they used to play darts. She kept coming back to the number of cattle it would feed, but could not get an answer out of the estate agent and gave up.

Berks tried to propose soon after they acquired the rectory "what about us" Felicity knew well what he was saying but she was not going to settle for a half-baked proposal. What do you mean says she until he had to state it in the king's English, which was an improvement if still lacking in romance, but she gracefully accepted? This occurred outside the Wimpy Bar in Sligo, a less romantic place you could not find. Being the practical person she was and being so worried about mortgages she suggested an antique ring that they could get in an antique shop and it need not cost too much and Berks who was god's gift to agreeability nodded his head and so they were engaged four months after meeting and ready for the long road.

Going home to Donegal to introduce him to the parents was quite a task. Previously possible suitors that Felicity had produced, two to be exact were quickly dismissed by mother, one she labelled as mentally retarded although he was a science graduate from Trinity and the other was English and she quickly realised that Felicity was not really interested in him romantically and therefore he was not a threat. Berks arrived to collect Felicity in a dreadful checked shirt and straight away she realised it was not going to go down well but then she decided so be it, whatever will be will be and they set off. The air was frosty at home and it was not all due to the cold, but they made the best of it and it was a short visit. At this stage, Felicity realised that no matter who she produced he would not reach her mother's high standard. They went out to the local hotel on the Saturday evening and her mother said she was asked by one of the snobby neighbours if that man, namely Berks, was with Felicity and who was he. This was repeated to Felicity by her mother in a tone leaving no doubt that the checked shirt had not reached acceptable standards.

Things moved on rapidly after that. Felicity was called to do a locum for a GP who was ill and so her career was launched. It was shortly after this that she started as an assistant in Berks small town to a very upright and generous G.P. who treated her fairly and due to him she got excellent training. Twenty house calls a day was the norm and alternate nights on duty. The G.Ps wife was a very generous but domineering woman who had caused two previous assistants to leave. Felicity tried to ignore her as much as possible, aware that her heart was in the right place and grateful to her for getting accommodation for her in the town. A year later Felicity got her own practice in Geevagh which she accepted as well as Ballymote was extremely busy and work was daily from 9 am until 7 or eight p.m. in the evening with on-call every second night including weekends, all of which her boss shared equally but Felicity felt there must be more to life than work, work and more work. It was really brought home to her one day when Berks was going to the races and she had to stay at home. The people in her new area Geevagh were often described by Felicity as the salt of the earth. She loved them, respected them, and never sought more lucrative pastures ending up spending 42 years attending to the flock. It was situated at the bottom of the Arigna mountains and was 17 miles from where she lived.
They set the date for the wedding and then looked for a venue her preference being Portnablagh but mother said no way so it was decided to have it in the Great Northern in Bundoran as it would be about halfway between Ballymote and Portnablagh and use the church in Drumcliffe, Yeats own country   One of Felicity's Uncles was seated in the Yeats church waiting for the wedding not realising it was the protestant church They were able to use Berks sports car as well as her friends Doreen car

for the church and a great day was had by all. Eventually her Father said it was time for the married couple to go at midnight that night.

They were booked into the Dunraven Arms in Mullingar so it was a two-hour drive and when they got there a rugby celebration was going on and Berks was terrified that anyone would recognise him. Their bedroom was not on-suite and they got locked in and had to send for reception to get them out. Life was never simple. They were off the next day to Istanbul in Turkey on their honeymoon.

The temperatures were so high in Turkey that the first thing they did was throw open the windows of their room not knowing anything about mosquitos until the following morning when they discovered that they were bitten from head to toe. They took off their wedding rings, talked to nobody and set off to explore Istanbul. It was a time in Turkey that if Berks moved away from Felicity she was quickly surrounded by men. Visitors were thin on the ground. Locals were friendly, too much so at times. As they were going for a trip on the Bosporus they met a local who tagged on to them and Berks spent a long time explaining about Christmas in Ireland, but he was a Muslim and did not know what Christmas was. On another occasion, they saw a bus going to Ankara and decided on the spur of the moment to jump on it and visit Ankara. When the bus got to Ankara their appearance was greeted with great excitement as visitors from the West were a rare species. Unfortunately, the natives had little or no English and did not understand hotel or accommodation so in desperation Felicity said they wanted the centre and one bright spark seemed to understand and off they went in a taxi only to be dropped at this so-called hotel which turned out to be a brothel with blue lights and the most basic of bedrooms but it was a place for the night and it was cheap.

On their return, they boarded the bus which had four seats in a row and as Felicity had the window on the way coming Berks was to have it on the way back. A big delay and much discourse was going on with looks being directed to them where they were sitting eventually 4 officials boarded the bus came straight down to them took both of them out of their seats, put Felicity next to the window then Berks in beside her, it transpired that as Felicity had short sleeves on she could not sit next to a Muslim.

On return, they had their fabulous old rectory and were so excited about doing it up. They spent weekends going to auctions to get it furnished and this opened a whole new interest in antiques and old furniture. Mother was very generous with the lolly to improve things. It was an extremely busy life. Berks was an undertaker, owned a pub and ran a farm. Felicity was often out until ten at night doing calls, she was on duty every second night. . As well as working in Geevagh she also held a surgery in Ballymote in Berks pub by converting a few rooms in the bar as her surgery. The joke was if you went to the doctor and she was late you could have a drink in the pub while you were waiting for the doctor who saw you and she finished you off so that Berks could do the undertaking.

Life was not all work, they took foreign holidays to places like Russia. They saw a cheap holiday to Russia via Scotland. To get to Scotland they went to Donegal where you could get a bus which was reasonably priced that brought workmen to Scotland to save the potato crop. When the people on the bus asked Felicity and Berks where they were going, and they said Russia there was no more talk on the bus after that. Russia was austere and it was impossible to move around much except on organised tours. The group they were with from Scotland were a communist cell and when they got a few jars loudly condemned rugby players, horse trainers and supporters so Felicity and Berks kept quiet. At night the Russians were paid to come into the hotel to dance and this was to show the tourists what a grand place Russia was.

On another occasion, they decided to visit an outlying town and were queuing at the bus stop but were quickly surrounded and told it was out of bounds. They were encouraged to go to talks in the evening to enlighten them about communism which they politely declined.
Shops couldn't care less if you never bought anything in their stores. Service in the restaurants was slow and unfriendly. The whole atmosphere was cold and unhelpful. It was amazing how no one ever smiled when they were dealing with you. This was back in 1975 when

Russia was still under strict communist rule. They also visited Kyiv and Socie on the black sea which was under Russian rule at that time. Later Felicity read the book The shoemaker and his daughter by Conor O Cleary which portrayed life in Russia during this era and it equated with what Berks and Felicity saw and experienced.

CHAPTER SIX PREGNANCY AND CHILDREN
****

After a year at last Felicity got pregnant and they were so excited as Felicity very much wanted a big family but unfortunately, she decided to clean out the front of the car while still driving and ended up in the drain alongside the road. Shortly after this, she had a miscarriage and much disappointment but as the old G.P. said at least now you know you can get pregnant. Mother who belonged to another era told people she was indisposed although she had a miscarriage after Felicity was born. but this was never mentioned. One more secret that she was not perfect and fertility was a bad word. One year later she was pregnant again and because of the heart murmur was advised to have the baby in Dublin. Her consultant there was a very austere man who would not answer any questions or give any information. At one of her antenatal visits, he was taking her medical history, when he asked her did she smoke and Felicity who was nervous of him said no thank you whereupon he rose a foot off the chair and exclaimed that he was not offering her one. Many of her colleagues who knew the consultant and heard this story thought it was hilarious. He was known as the young Hitler and one night there was a party at the doctor's residency and the bouncer at the door did not know this consultant and refused to let him in causing great trouble with the hospital authorities.

Felicity enjoyed good health during the pregnancy but morning sickness was a problem which seemed to hit her on her morning journey to Geevagh and had her stopping on route to puke. This proved problematic as many cars passing recognized her car and stopped to offer help so she spent her journey turning up side roads to avoid these helpful gestures.

Not everyone was happy being pregnant. This was brought home to Felicity when she got called to a patient who was due at the same time as her and on giving the patient the good news that she was starting labour the response was a mouth full of curses, threatening vengeance on hubby and declaring loud and clear that she did not want this baby, leaving Felicity dumbfounded.

Felicity's child was born on the 28th of November which was the day that Felicity was admitted to the hospital. On admission, she was told that the head was high, and she could be many days waiting but went into labour that night. When she called the nurse to say she was in labour the nurse said do not be silly that it was a reaction to an emergency that they had just dealt with in the ward and she gave Felicity a sleeping tablet which she threw in the bin. After the nurse left, she decided that she was in a hospital, she was safe and got on with it. She did not call the nurse again until four am. which was six hours later. The nurse who was a real grumpy spice said OK I will examine you and then it was straight to the labour ward where she had a forceps delivery at five am. Dr O Driscoll her obstetrician was called in and he gave some instructions to the nurses who set up trolly, stirrups etc When Felicity asked him what he was going to do he just looked at her and walked away. He was setting up for a forceps delivery but not something that should concern the patient. The new staff came on at six am when she was due to go back to the ward. She again got another grumpy nurse who said get down off that trolley and find your slippers. The floor looked miles below to Felicity and she was so vulnerable, but she managed to get into the wheelchair to go back to the ward with her gorgeous baby son in her lap having been a model patient.

There was no maternity leave for us at that time so not only did they not get paid leave, but you had to pay a locum to look after your patients, so babies were a dear commodity. Felicity took eight weeks leave while many of her colleagues only took a week or two as it was all they could afford. After coming home she was put into a single room done up by Berks; it even had a draft excluder at the door. Felicity had definite ideas on feeding, going for breast and establishing a time schedule. After the child had cried for half an hour, mother burst into the room and told her to stop her nonsense and give the child a bottle and not to be like the itinerants whereupon Felicity told her she could go home tomorrow. On day two Felicity moved back into the double bed with Berks and life settled down.

The rectory with its name of being haunted inspired Felicity to have the station mass in the house and every last person in the station area came as they were interested in seeing the inside of the house. Maybe they thought the ghost might appear. Any evil spirits were truly banished after the station. Mother came to help, and her job was to mind the baby of nine months and Felicity could not believe how nervous she was after teaching infants all her life. Station masses were a rural thing going back to the olden times and everyone was expected to take the station when it was their turn. It involved much painting and sprucing up of the house as well as supplying food and drink and put great pressure on some families. Everyone paid money which went to the priest, so the poor house owner was the only one that suffered.

Berks started keeping horses and training show jumpers, both he and his brother Michael enjoyed it very much. They had ready stables at the rectory, and it was great to have Michael coming and going as he was a firm favourite with the children. He had a big heart and a pocket full of money. It was not only the children who loved him but many other people who were helped by him. Training horses involved buying young horses, breaking them, training them as show jumpers, and entering them in jumping competitions all around the west of Ireland generally at weekends. Felicity would go with him and later all the children together with a picnic regardless of the weather. Felicity knew that in order to make the most of life she needed to get involved and follow the competitions around the west of Ireland in the horsey world. Out of this, she got a job as a doctor at the Dublin horse show held every summer where she had a VIP seat and prayed that no one would come off their horse she would have to run into the arena to check that they were not seriously injured. In all her years doing the show she only once had to go into the arena to a nine-year-old who had come off her pony and when Felicity reached her and asked if she was hurt was told to fuck off by the child whose frustration was palpable. At the Dublin horse show one child would carry her bag of tricks into the V.I.P stand, a much-coveted job that had to be shared from year to year. She always talks about the youngest Eymard carrying the bag which was almost as big as himself.

Felicity at this stage had started to fulfil her dream of a big family and number one son was followed by number two, a daughter who came two weeks early so Felicity had no time to go to Dublin so it was into her old consultant friend in the local hospital. The evening she went into labour Berks had gone swimming with a friend, Felicity had a large curry which was one of her fads in pregnancy and her waters broke,
When she got into the hospital, she went out of labour so the consultant gave her a room over in isolation so that she could get some rest and the nurse gave her a sleeping tablet which she threw in the bin.
She went to sleep and woke up in the early morning to discover that she was back in labour and that the head was there waiting to be born, the bell would not work and she was frantic trying to shout for a nurse, When they came they wanted to hold back the head until the consultant came and Felicity kept telling them to deliver the child, eventually the consultant arrived and the little girl was born with the cord around the neck but was healthy and strong. It is well known that if things are to go wrong it will often be a medic who is the victim.

Another little girl was born a year later but went two weeks overdue. Felicity was in Dublin waiting and not too patiently when eventually she went into labour she had to queue up at 4 am to be admitted with six other expectant mothers in the month of March to the National Maternity Hospital Holles St. Some of the patients queuing with her were in sandals and had their bits of belongings wrapped in newspaper. Again labour stopped when she was admitted so they decided to induce her by putting up a Pitocin drip and rupturing the membranes a labour Felicity will never forget all is well that ends well and she had her two lovely daughters whom she called her balls of fluff and she loved them dearly.

Her fourth child was born a big healthy eight-pound boy she called Heber. After three days she noticed he was not feeling well, and she crept up to the nursery to check his temperature, but it was normal. She voiced her concerns to the nurse who told the consultant so on his rounds had a look at the baby over the blanket and told her that he looked perfectly healthy and not to be fussing but by the evening Felicity knew all was not well and again she went to the nurse who took one look at the baby and whisked him off to the neonatal unit. It was quickly diagnosed that he had some version of congenital heart disease and he was transferred to Crumlin hospital where he was found to have hypoplastic left ventricle, a condition where the left side of the heart is not properly formed and it is not compatible with life.

She found it an overwhelming grief to lose a child much worse than a parent or any other death. To walk out of the hospital with no bundle in your arms. To pass the lake in Mullingar where she always feeds the babies on the way home. Because of her heart murmur, she was not at home when the baby was buried, it was all over when she got there, and this may have made it even harder. It was three months before she ventured out to a social night at which she was asked to dance but broke down in the middle of it much to her partner's distress, but he understood, and Berks brought her home.

She said it was like a hollow in your stomach that is never filled. She found it strange how difficult, good female friend of hers had sympathising or talking about Heber which was the name she called him. She waited ten weeks before going back for her postnatal check-up. When she walked into the consultant the first thing he said to her was how is the baby which had her in floods of tears again. You are not still upset over the baby, I had forgotten he said. It really showed the difference between the male and female psyche. Felicity got rapidly pregnant again although you cannot replace a baby you have lost with another one.

Another son was born one year later but came early so she had to go to the local hospital. She noticed the consultant's face turning white when he examined her, it transpired that the cord had prolapsed down ahead of the baby and when it hits fresh air it stops supplying blood to the baby. It is one of the acute emergencies of delivery so she was rushed to the theatre and he had the baby out in eight minutes hale and hearty. The anaesthetist's hand who was putting her to sleep was shaking as he was giving her the anaesthetic because she had told him that she had a massive curry just before coming in, a food she was very partial to during pregnancy. A day later the consultant was whispering to Berks at the door of the ward saying that he would try to get her a room but not to say anything. Poor Berks would not tell her what they had been talking about so she thought this child must also have something wrong, only when she was on the verge of hysteria did Berks tell her it was about a room, something she had little interest in.

She got a wonderful lady who was a second mother to the children called Aine. She was a kind loving person married to P.J. who was also an attentive caring person and the children loved them to bits. They remain part of the family to this day. Apart from the love and care she gave them she was a refined lady who gave them a bit of finesse sadly lacking in Felicity's make up. The children missed out on grandparents as the paternal parents were dead before the marriage and the maternal parents died in the first three years of the marriage, so the parents were orphans but had each other and their children.

Felicity continued in her own practice in the remote mining area 17 miles from her home and she worked there mornings and kept her old practice in Ballymote going as well. She worked 9 to 1 pm in the remote mining practice, took the afternoon off to be with the kids and worked again in her hometown from 8 to 10 pm. when the children were gone to bed. Her new area was populated by patients who she described as the salt of the earth and she never wanted to leave although the day she started in the area she called on the parish priest out of courtesy. He stood tall and imperious and said is it you they are sending to us now, obviously he was not impressed.

Felicity and Berks were not involved in any parish activities so they sat down to see what they could do to spread a little happiness, their conclusion was that they both loved children they had a big house and they would adopt a child to love, rear, educate and give a loving home to the best of their ability and so they applied through the regular channels to adopt a child. Many meetings later with references produced, visits to the house, spot checks etc, they were passed. Eventually, they were asked if there was anything they had to say or request and Felicity said they would like to get the child at a week old but there was no way their request could be honoured as the mother might take back the child. Felicity's assurance that if this happened there would be no problem fell on deaf ears. It had to be 8 weeks a stupid rule if the adoptive parents signed a consent form.

They had to go to Dublin when the adopted child was 6 months old to finalise the adoption. Felicity was so afraid they would ask her if she was pregnant and take the child off her, but all went smoothly. At the time the adoption came about Felicity got hepatitis A and, on the day, she collected her son Evan she was still yellow and the rule was that he had to be christened before she took him home. Their friendly neighbours stood for him and it was straight home as Felicity was not well enough to go out celebrating however it was done a few weeks later and Felicity took 8 weeks off. This beautiful child made a family of five and they decided that was it but nature had other ideas and two months later Felicity found herself pregnant again.

7 months later Eymard, another boy, arrived into the world at only five pounds. As Felicity had a significant bleed on New Year's Eve, she always thought that Eymard might have been a twin. All her other babies were over 8 lbs. He was a breech presentation, a fact that caused disagreement among four different consultants. Eventually they asked Felicity how would she like to be delivered and she said what was safest for the baby and so the decision was a section. There was such a thrill walking out the door of Holles St Hospital with her bonnie baby boy and stopping outside Mullingar at Lough Innel to feed him on the way home.

CHAPTER 7 MEDICAL HISTORY
****

Felicity applied to become a trainer of young G.P.s especially relevant as she worked in such a rural area in splendour isolation. She felt it would keep her on her toes and maybe the teacher background was coming out in spite of her fight against it in her youth. It proved to be a very good experience.Initially, she would get them to sit in with her for the first week. One individual on his first day started writing furiously and she was fascinated to know what he was writing about. He informed her that he was writing down all the things that needed to be done to improve the surgery, like what said Felicity - well a nice white sheet for the examination couch, an excellent idea said Felicity, I am sure you will find a suitable one when you go home this evening. That was the last she heard about improvements.

Training involved one afternoon a week attending trainers' meetings and attendance at trainers' workshops two or three times a year and although it was intensely academic it had its fun times. Felicity would always say it was necessary to have an outlet other than general practice to keep your enthusiasm up. G.P. Felicity felt was rather humdrum with only about one in six patients needing treatment but as her husband would say where else will they be asked how they are feeling, or where else will they meet the neighbours for a chin wag, it added excitement to their day, you would wonder could these needs be taken care of in some other way less medical and more social not to talk about the economic aspect.

It was after a hectic day in the surgery getting everyone fed and rushing up and down stairs that Felicity set off to a trainer's workshop in Sligo. Six miles from home she felt the sudden speeding up of her heart rate with an abnormal erratic beat. She knew it was a condition called atrial fibrillation and she was also aware that she was quite dizzy with it, so she drove very carefully stopping and pulling into the side of the road if she saw a lorry coming. Her plan was to drive to the next town and go into the G.P there but when she got that far she said I will go a little further and go into my trainee who lived on the route. Again on reaching there, she said I may as well go as far as the hospital. As she was pulling into the hospital one of the consultants pulled in behind her. When she tried to get out of the car, she could not walk so she had to call the consultant Dr Healy who got her into coronary care and got a heart tracing which showed the atrial fibrillation.

After a short time, she reverted to a normal rhythm and told Dr Healy who had rescued her that she was going to ring Berks to come and collect her and that she was grand. Dr Healy knew her too well and said you have no notion of ringing him and he was right, so he insisted on following her out the road to make sure she got home safely.
Felicity knew it was D-day and she needed consultant care and treatment which she sought in her old Alma Mater with a cardiologist. He diagnosed a tight pulmonary valve which is the valve of the large blood vessel going from the heart to the lungs. He tried to dilate it by angiogram and balloon dilation, but it was not successful, and the only solution was to proceed to open heart surgery. A hard decision with the youngest of the six children only seven years old but the alternative was a no-no so surgery was scheduled. This involved locums, and childcare, although hubby was brilliant, but he could not do it all and a date was set.

Felicity got a bad head cold just prior to surgery but decided to say nothing about it. Her cardiologist gave her great encouragement and eventually she was on the table under Mr Freddy Woods. What she felt was that he can work wonders with children with congenital heart defects so as she was an adult hers should be easy. At surgery it was discovered that she had more than just pulmonary valve narrowing, there was also a ventricular septal defect which is a hole between the ventricles of the heart and a septal defect between the atrial chambers all compensating each other but very tricky surgery.

After surgery, Felicity developed a respiratory tract infection affecting the lungs and as a result, was unable to get off the respirator for more than ten days hanging in there between life and death with all Ballymote praying for her, organised by her friend Nancy Tighe. Hubby was up to his eyes in childcare, The hospital was not impressed that he was so far

away in Sligo when things were at a critical stage. Slow but sure she came out of it, but it was a long time to be intubated more than ten days. Normally they would do a tracheotomy if you were on a respirator for that length to prevent any damage around the back of the throat.
Felicity will tell how disorientated she was after surgery due to the intrathecal morphine she was getting for pain relief. She saw a neighbour in the bed next to her with a purple bedspread over his bed and ducks walking all over it. A friend's husband was coming in to give a grind to one of the nurse's sons but Felicity saw the son coming in with earphones and jiving and she was telling the nurse not to waste her money as her son was a loser. She thought she saw the I.R.A. surrounding the ward and Felicity was so worried that when they would break in, she could not run That and many other hallucinations real to this day. But they were not at all pleasant so why would anyone want morphine?

After, recovery was fairly rapid. She kept complaining of something stuck in her throat but no one paid any heed. At last, she was discharged and went to the local private hospital for ten days before facing the troops at home. Within three weeks of getting home Felicity was back at work full time and three months later she was organising a campsite in France and they set off with the six children to France in a Volkswagen golf. The raw feeling in the neck persisted and after ten months she went to an E.N.T. consultant but he said it was due to nerve damage and not to worry about it, however, after 12 months she was seriously compromised with breathing and ended up having to have an emergency tracheotomy in the Eye and Ear Hospital in Dublin due to narrowing in the posterior glottic area which was a complication of being intubated for a long time after her surgery.
The Eye and Ear hospital is a very old establishment where the wards are a mixture of males and females, most disconcerting to wake up in the morning to see 2 beady eyes looking over at you from a bed across the room. She was lucky to have a classmate working there who was very attentive to her. One of the doctors came to tell her how excited her consultant was about her condition and that he was going to practise on the stiffs over Easter and try to correct her narrowing. This caused alarm bells to ring for Felicity and she knew that she needed to seek help

elsewhere, a fact she found out from a very helpful junior doctor who told her she should get out of the hospital in Dublin and try across the water. She had already reached this conclusion after the story of the surgeon going to practise on the stiffs.

Felicity went to London but was told to live with the tracheotomy, a condition that did not suit Felicity's lifestyle of swimming and hard work. Defeat was not part of her make up and she took to the net to see what was going on in the wider world. She discovered that they were correcting it in Boston and in the Mayo Clinic in Minnesota. As she had contacts in the Mayo Clinic she set about getting further information. Her Irish consultant when he heard it said he had a good friend in the Mayo clinic and that he would write to him. Felicity was not impressed that he only came up with this information when she had all the research done. This is a problem you will encounter in Ireland where consultants are loath to refer their patients to someone with greater expertise.
Felicity had a good friend whose Uncle worked in the Mayo clinic as a cardiologist and she also knew a few of her classmates who had gone there so there was steady progress toward getting there. At this stage, she still had her tracheotomy but could cover it for short periods and she was able to continue full-time work.

The Mayo was arranged, the date set, but no visa got and no progress on a visa so a first in her life she sought the help of a politician and had her visa in two days. To give her peace of mind Berks had to stay with the children and although two good colleagues offered to go with her, she set off on her solo mission. The journey was long, she had said nothing about the tracheotomy as she was afraid the airline would refuse to take her. Halfway across the Atlantic the person next to her asked her if she had a tracheotomy. Felicity nearly freaked out and said how did you know but this person was a physiotherapist who worked in an intensive care unit in America and they were able to have a good chat for the rest of the journey.

Initially, the H.S.E. went guarantor for her but the customs were not impressed to find she was going for surgery at the Mayo clinic and only had 2000 pounds with her. She first stayed with a classmate Brendan

Moor. He and his wife Mary made her very welcome. The first day she had appointments all over the place to be accessed for surgery after which she decided not to go back to the house to give her friends a chance and not to have to cook for her so she ate out but her hosts were freaking out thinking she was lost and Brendan was ringing consultants clinics etc. to see if anyone had seen her.

The surgery was severe, she was wheeled down to a holding bay where there were 70 individual bays all containing patients awaiting surgery, it is the second biggest hospital in the world. At surgery, they lasered the area that was narrowed, grafted it with buccal membrane and stented it. The pain was severe but especially in the mouth where they had got the buccal membrane from. She was only kept in the hospital for 3 days, Felicity felt very lonely so far from home and depending on friends although they were so good to her, but she felt so tearful every time they came to visit her. After discharge she went back to her friend's uncle, he was from Ireland and worked in the clinic and his wife who was German was a psychiatrist called Ruth.

Felicity could only take liquidised food and even that was a struggle. There was a constant worry that the tracheotomy might block, and Ruth got a nebuliser and a humidifier for her which helped. She tried to help in the house as much as she could, polishing the silver, ironing old wrapping paper for reuse, and doing a little cooking. The weather was good most of the time and she took long walks. Also, the Irish community rallied around her, Cynthia Malloy, the Sullivan family and others, she re attended the clinic on a regular basis. She made many friends that she would drop in on not realising it was not the done thing there unlike Ireland.

It was a long lonely time and she was almost four weeks there before they were prepared to let her go home still with her tracheotomy, but it was to be taken out after six weeks. It was an episode in her life which showed how kind and helpful people are when you are in trouble. Felicity always had a problem accepting help and invited the family out for a meal before she went home to the most expensive restaurant she could find in Rochester. She insisted they take pre-dinner drinks and ordered lavishly from the menu only to discover that Dr Connolly, her host, had pre-paid for all.

The whole experience had cost over 17 thousand and the H.S. E had paid eight thousand and the V.H.I had paid two thousand, the rest she had to pay herself. As it resulted from a medical error due to being intubated too long it should have been paid for by the authorities. She still had over 50 per cent narrowing and was warned to go to the hospital if she got a severe respiratory tract infection such as a bad sore throat. She could walk any distance on the flat but could not do hills or steps. After she came back from America she heard from the H.S.E to refund the money she had paid but she informed them that it was due to a medical error and if they persist in pursuing the money she would be forced to take legal action and would get millions from them ... There was no further communication from the H.S.E.

The narrowing was to stay with her for the rest of her life, preventing her from climbing any hills or heights and this prevented her from taking part in many activities that her friends did. If she went on medical conferences with her GP colleagues which occurred yearly in various countries she would tell the others that she was not going on the walks and when they were gone she would follow slowly which she was able to do. Her worst night ever was on Aruba Island where she had gone to meet her son who was bringing a yacht home from Australia to Ireland. She got a bad sore throat and there was no hospital on the island and the only G.P. went off to the mainland at night. She will never forget sitting up all night with a boiling kettle to give steam and might have said a few prayers. A very caring E.N.T consultant Mr Choo gave her an emergency tracheostomy tube and a letter to have with her in case she ran into trouble abroad or even at home and if she had to go to A and E they might have a problem finding a tracheostomy tube.

CHAPTER SEVEN FAMILY HOLIDAYS
****

Holidays were very important to Felicity and Berks and they did the campsites in France eight years in a row. A prelude to going to France was staying overnight in Jurys Hotel in Cork all eight in one room, it had a swimming pool and a jacuzzi and was a great start to their holiday while still on Irish soil. On the ferry they all had bunks and the children really enjoyed the boat.

Felicity and Berks tried to get an upmarket meal when the children went to bed on the ferry, Felicity was anxious to get familiar with a few wines so she would have a name of one that she liked and they got one on the ferry called Pies Porter, in order to remember it Felicity called it pissing Porter and never forgot that name and she would be able to appear knowledge by requesting it in company. As was inevitable one or other of the children would arrive down to the dining room with a question in the middle of the meal. Arrival in France off the ferry was at 6 am on a Sunday morning so they were well down through France before the traffic got heavy They would set off in the golf car all eight of them and due to numbers, it was all picnics to spread the cash.

Felicity hit on a great plan, she divided the children into three pairs and offered a prize of 50 euros to the pair that produced the best meal in the evening on a budget of 20 euros and another prize for the couple that left the mobile home the cleanest. The competition was fierce and there had to be a second and third prize. As they got bigger they recruited a few French girls to help especially with the cooking.

One year they decided to do Lido De Jesolo in Italy and started by staying in a campsite in Wales where it rained nonstop and everyone got a vomiting bug. The last to get it was Evan and he vomited all over Berks. The only solution was to book into a b and b and try to wash some of the clothes before setting off in the morning by bus to Italy. This journey turned out to be a marathon with heavy traffic and high temperatures. On arrival, they discovered they only had 10 days as they had wasted a lot of time travelling, despite this, they had a good holiday and enjoyed St. Mark's Square and the boats in Venice.

Another year they went to St Tropez. Life was never dull with the six, they toured all around. Getting on a bus one day to go to Nice, after 4 of the children had got on the bus, the passengers were making signs to cut off Berks head, big families were uncommon then in France.

Euro Disney in Paris was another adventure preceded by Berks deciding to sit in the boot of the car and squashing a 5 ltr bottle of cooking oil that burst so it was all over him and the boot of the car. They camped in a large campsite outside Paris on the Seine River and safety was a major problem as the children were used to complete freedom which had to be curtailed.

As time progressed and they grew out of family holidays, she changed the venue to the 1st of January for a week and as mum was paying, they were very popular holidays and life was good. Felicity loved having all the family together. On these new year holidays, they did Malta, Tunisia, Agadir, and Spain and it was great to have the adult children interacting with you and with each other. This was a whole new ball game as now with older teenagers and nightlife high in the reckoning there was a great opportunity for example and advice to be given as well as mutual enjoyment to be had by all.

As the pension is so bad from the health board for G.Ps they must try and put in place other sources of income for when they retire so, Felicity and Berks who were good savers invested as much as they could afford in property like apartments in Dublin 4, Galway and Sligo. Berks did a lot of the work himself on these properties, some were successful others not so rewarding. By getting them well-managed they were relatively trouble-free. One apartment that Felicity got in Galway when Berks was away on holiday had to be seen before the estate agent would sell it to her so Felicity speeded off to Galway between clinics, met the estate agent at the site, sat on a rock in the grounds and counted out the money for the deposit and rushed back to Sligo to be in time for the next surgery. It was a first for the estate agent, doing business on the rocks. The children were great but challenging. They all went off to boarding school at 12-13 and all were happy, in fact, the school principal in the national school said they were the happiest children in the school but where were their coats? They hated wearing coats and often had to have their clothes changed at school after getting wet en route.

The boys went to Galbally College in Ballinasloe and the girls went to St Michael's in Claremorris and it was a successful time in their lives although one hated it and two were full of defilement like one tying a rope on the roof of the collage and then anchoring it to the ground forty feet below He then used a belt which was plastic to slide down the forty feet, but the belt was only plastic and rapidly broke, luckily, he landed in a skip of rubbish as otherwise, he would have got killed.
One of the girls set off the fire alarm in the middle of the night and guided the pupils out onto the roof. The nuns were muttering for weeks that they did not think they could bring back Felicity's daughter in September unless she changed but it all settled eventually. Baruch the oldest boy followed in his father's footsteps and was captain of the rugby team in his final year in Garbally.

Eventually, Felicity and Berks were on their own and everyone had flown the nest. One had sailed a 32 ft yacht back from Australia which took up to two and a half years as he had to come home every six months or so to try to make money to continue his epic voyage. He managed to get the boat by investing in Elan shares which went up by a multiple of ten and the boat became a reality. Life was never calm with this son as he then managed to be shipwrecked off Norfolk Island and had to put up a mayday call. He was rescued by the authorities on the island and their care, help, and advice are a tribute to all that is admirable about human nature.

Baruch spent the next year and a half rebuilding his boat with a book in one hand and a hammer in the other and invaluable advice from the locals. He was not alone as his girlfriend took a leave of absence of one year to help him. He set out eventually with two of a crew, one of whom went psychiatric after a day or two of sailing and wanted to go back but was duly deposited on an island which meant diverting 60 to 70 miles to drop him. He lay on the bottom of the boat, refused to move and offered 2000 euros if Baruch would go back. The inboard engine failed just prior to taking off from Australia and was duly dumped and a small outboard got to enable them to get in and out of ports On his long voyage home Felicity flew out and joined him in the Azores, Aruba and Argentina. She would always say what friendly helpful people were in the marinas and contrary to public image were in no way wealthy good timers.

Her eyes opened wide one night as a fellow traveller said how lucky her son was when the boat went on fire, the story being that Baruch thought he smelt gas and proceeded to light a match so up went the flames, luckily the girlfriend had checked the fire extinguisher and it was working. His homecoming was lonely as he eventually sailed into Mullaghmore at 3 am in the morning and there was only one loyal friend to meet him. Now Felicity looks out in the morning and thanks the lord as she sees the boat on dry land.

CHAPTER NINE GENERAL PRACTICE
****

Felicity practised eventually at the foot of the Arigna mountains near the coal mines. On one of her first night calls she met all these men coming down the mountain with black faces and did not realise they were coming from the Arigna mines. At that time the I.R.A. were very active and she was not sure what was going on. On another occasion, she got a house call and she set off but as she was driving on the back road she saw this donkey and cart coming towards her with no driver, thinking that he was asleep in the cart she started to blow the horn to no avail and it dawned on her that the donkey was not going to stop so she leapt out of the car and grabbed a stick but on the donkey came and she ended up getting a big scrape all along the side of the car.

One of her patients was complaining of pain in his testicles and that the previous doctor had said it was because the wife would not let him near her. Having ruled out any pathology Felicity in her wisdom decided that the wife was probably afraid of pregnancy and as it was the time when condoms could only be got on prescription she said she would give him a prescription for condoms and the wife might be ok with that. When he was leaving he turned back and asked who takes these me or the wife so he had to come back and be suitably tutored. There was a follow-up to this when the wife stormed in and read the riot act for introducing those filthy things into her house. Felicity in retrospect felt she was at fault knowing that particular family.

She delivered premature babies out on the mountains that were barely 3 lbs in weight and on one occasion having delivered a premature baby weighing 3 lbs she sent for an ambulance, a nurse and an incubator. When they arrived she handed over the baby to the nurse who put him in the incubator while Felicity attended to the mum who had high blood pressure and there was a danger of convulsions. It meant travelling in the ambulance with a syringe full of Valium at the ready When they reached the hospital, the nurse had failed to turn on the incubator and the child was suffering from hypothermia. All survived to tell the tale.

One Wednesday she was called to Arigna to treat a severe asthmatic as she was covering for another doctor who was a politician and had to be in the Dail every Wednesday. When she got there the young girl was collapsed and cyanosed, Felicity hit her with everything in the book including steroids, aminophylline, adrenaline and others and gradually got her back from near death. She decided at this stage to drive her to Roscommon hospital although Felicity was 7 months pregnant herself and it was January with slippery roads. The relatives decided not to let her go to the hospital and Felicity would say that if they had not jumped out of her way that night she would have run them down. One of her main concerns was that poor Berks would be out of his mind with worry about her as the roads were slippery and she was so long away. When eventually Felicity got home Berks was happily snoring in his bed having sweet dreams. This was a time when there were no mobile phones.

The local priest was not enamoured of her but one morning one of his parishioners collapsed at mass and he had to send for her. Felicity noted that the patient was hyperventilating so she asked the priest for a paper bag which she got the patient to breathe in and out of and she was well again within minutes. She informed the priest that it was a miracle not due to God but to her.

When one of Felicities daughters was getting married Felicity looked at a new community football clubhouse that had been built in Geevagh on the football pitch and as the whole top floor was given over to a restaurant she felt it was ideal for a wedding but her daughter thought otherwise and eventually picked the most expensive place in the area Cromlaugh Lodge but at least it was local and eventually was a super choice as it ticked all the boxes and even had a great breakfast the following morning to which anyone was welcome to come to.

The journey to work in Geevagh was over 17 miles and to maximise the use of time Felicity got Russian tapes to play on the route as she was bringing her firstborn with her every day to Geevagh to be minded and she reckoned if he heard these tapes he would end up with fluent Russian., She used to go home by Lough Key as she thought that she would have him swimming at a year old if she put him in the lake every day. He was not swimming before 4 and he never learned Russian.

Life had its ups and downs Felicity's youngest child Eymard had followed in the footpaths of the others, getting his degree in college and then heading off to see the world assuring his mother that he would meet others in hostels and make friends along the way. He was a guy who liked to take risks and do all the things like bungee jumping, ab sailing etc. just to prove that he could. Eventually, he arrived in Australia where some of his friends were and Felicity breathed a sigh of relief. To extend his visa he went to work in the outback on one of the big farms picking fruit. There are massive farms in the outback where it is difficult to get workmen, so the government gives extended visas to students or other workers who are prepared to give their time there.
Initially, he was complaining about the isolation of it but all that stopped, and Felicity was amazed when he opted to stay on after his stint was finished. Eventually, he made his way to Sydney where his pals were and got a job in construction so Felicity thought she could eventually relax but one fatal Saturday night out with the pals he opted to go to the ATM machine rather than go back with the boys and while crossing the road was hit twice first by a taxi and then by another taxi coming behind. The road had six lanes and he sustained catastrophic injuries, head injuries, ruptured liver and spleen and three spinal injuries and was brought into St Vincent Hospital where they did boreholes to the skull and he was put on a respirator in the intensive care unit.
Felicity and her oldest son Baruch travelled to Australia to the intensive care unit where Eymard was on life support, a journey like no other. They were driven to Dublin by her son Evan and his wife Gillian and it was great to get their support.

The pals had left their jobs to keep a vigil at the hospital by his bedside and Felicity was extremely grateful to them. There was a girl there also called Eveline who was from Amsterdam, but Felicity didn't know her. It transpired that she was Eymard's girlfriend of six months which had not been mentioned in any of his letters or phone calls home. Her son's friend Mark Ryan had arranged accommodation and all the hospital staff were so kind and helpful.

His injuries were absolutely not compatible with life and the terrible decision had to be made when to turn off the machine that was keeping him alive. He was always a daredevil doing bungee jumps, paragliding, diving, snowboarding, surfing, surviving all until the alcohol literally caused his death leaving a sad perpetual void behind him.

Felicity was agreeable to donate his organs, kidneys, lungs and heart a tiny spark in the whole sorry procedure. The doctors were so willing to give their time and advice and the fatal day arrived when the machine was turned off something that is beyond description but can be vaguely appreciated if you are a parent. Between putting up makeshift beds for them and giving them a pastoral care attendant, they were so well treated. After the machine was turned off, he took 5 short breaths on his own and that was it. Felicity was devastated and life would never be the same again but to fall apart would only detract from his memories. Baruch, the oldest son who was with her, was a rock of support.

The police were involved as it was a traffic accident. There were two police involved, a middle-aged man and a very young female officer, she was the only one that Felicity would say was so cruel to her in that she launched into a tirade about these young Irish boys drinking on a Saturday night and causing so much trouble. It was wounding to the core to have this upcast to a grieving mother in the circumstances.
After the organs were taken the body was sent to the morgue and Felicity had to identify him again, she found one of the hardest things of all as he looked so peaceful and all his curls had come back.
He was cremated after the organs were removed and all the Irish boys came to the cremation and a cousin who had also been travelling but came specially for it. He was a first cousin called Carol and gave a very nice few words at the service. There were two neighbours from Ballymote on holidays who also gave up their time to offer support. After the cremation, everyone went back to Dirty Nellies for food and drink and Felicity stuck it for a short time before escaping to be on her own.
The Irish consulate offered help and there was a Margaret Duggan who was an administrator with the Irish community and Fr Tom Deverau A Chaplain with the Irish community who were most helpful to organise the cremation and were on hand twenty-four hours a day for advice and

help. Felicity carried the ashes home and had no problems at the airports. They travelled with ETIHAD airlines who upgraded them and gave them access to the V.I.P lounges at the stopovers.
It was an experience beyond description and one that Felicity would say takes a third of your life and replaces it with a cold heavy stone that never goes away but what got her through it was that she knew that he would want her to live on, be happy and do the best she could. To do otherwise would be letting him down so that is what she did, kept busy and left no room for reflection.

Her colleagues and friends were wonderful setting up a weekly meeting, and with her other children giving help and support, one day followed another and then one year followed another She erected a bench to Eymard in the local park and Baruch with the other siblings put up a plaque on the cliffs near Mullaghmore where Eymard used to surf. Felicity invited Eymard's girlfriend, Eveline, who was quite devastated by his death to visit her in Ireland when she came home, She flew into Knock airport and spent 4 days with her giving Felicity a chance to get to know her. Subsequently, one of Eymard's siblings Thecla invited Eveline and her mother to her wedding in Oxford. Felicity had never been told about this girlfriend, but it transpired that she had been with him in the outback and thence his reluctance to leave when his stint was finished. He leaves a sad perpetual void behind him.

Felicity's husband Berks as he was known was such a healthy man all his life and a great rugby player but he contracted pneumococcal meningitis when he was 71 years of age. Felicity was at a clinical conference in Trinity when he went into hospital sent in by Felicity's trainee who rang her and said she could find nothing much wrong with him, but the nurse was very insistent that she send him in. Felicity rang casualty but they were still doing tests on him and might keep him for the night so there were no major worries. When Felicity rang her son who had brought him in to tell him to go home he said they had sent for a consultant as Berks had collapsed and it turned out that he had pneumococcal meningitis and he was put into intensive care as there is a 70 per cent mortality rate with it. If he had been attending a g.p., he might have got the pneumococcal vaccine which is given at the same time as the flu vaccine to all over 65 but Berks wanted no trucking with doctors.

He survived the meningitis against all the odds but got kidney failure out of it and spent the next 9 years on dialysis. It was the pits of a life although Felicity sourced out where you could get dialysis on the continent and made sure he got on holidays but you never feel well on dialysis and things can go very wrong. On dialysis, the idea is to reduce the urea and creatinine levels in the blood which it does but only marginally and you still have the exhaustion and the lethargy of raised levels. The poor man was a bit of a saint and never complained. Felicity remembered the night he called her with breathlessness due to fluid retention and asked her if there was no injection she could give him for his breathing. She felt so useless and upset.

One night when he was on peritoneal dialysis the fistula burst and he called Felicity. When she jumped out of the bed the blood hit her in the face and when she put on the light it had hit the roof such was the pressure. Felicity who was in a flimsy nightdress and bursting to go to the loo applied strong pressure to the ruptured area to stop the blood. Eventually, she was able to keep one thumb on the bleeder and with the other hand reach the phone and ring 999 for an ambulance and her son for help. The ambulance was there in double quick time and Berks went off to the hospital. Normally when a fistula bursts the patient dies as no one knows what to do but luckily Felicity was there.

His life was so miserable at the end that it was a happy release when he died nine years later. During this incredibly hard time he attended Beaumont hospital and was treated very well by all the staff, bar the actual consultant, who refused to put him on the transplant list probably due to age which you are not allowed to say but is the only treatment that offers a glimmer of hope for a normal life. Cardiac problems followed kidney failure and eventually on the last day he got severe chest pain. Luckily his son Berchmans junior was visiting him that day and was in the hospital when he died.

CHAPTER 10 FRIENDS HOLIDAYS
****

As she was now retired, holidays became an annual event with plans to visit far-flung countries during the month of January. Her motto was to do it while the friends could walk, talk, climb and were compos mentis. Felicity was lucky to have four loyal friends who got on well together and they had like-minded interests and were financially able to spend the month of January exploring the universe. They started with India specifically Kerala as two of the group had done the usual tourist route of Delhi, Agra Jaipur e t c.

They were lucky to know a local chap that was working in Cochin who organised a driver with a jeep who was at their beck and call for three weeks and drove them all over Kerala. Their driver's name was Arun and he was a gem. You would see him in the morning washing the car from top to toe and then himself. They stayed in what is called government buildings which cost about ten euros a night and were treated to a top-rate breakfast cooked by three of the staff. Scrumptious omelettes, newly baked bread and all sorts of fruit. When this breakfast was served the staff stood looking at you while you ate it. They seemed to be the only people staying in these government buildings.

Before going to India Felicity had met a doctor that had worked in India and he advised her to take 250mg of ciprofloxacin every night to prevent Delhi belly i.e. vomiting and diarrhoea. Felicity and her companions were the only members of the group that didn't get the dreaded Delli belly.
At one stage they visited an ashram where the big fat hugging mama was, also known as Amana although she was on tour during their visit. It was only five euros for a full board and was an amazing experience. These ashrams are all over India and Felicity had heard about this one run by the big fat hugging mama who tours extensively, is reputed to have magic powers and is also thought to be extremely wealthy resulting from her American and European tours. They invited Arun, their driver, to book accommodation, but he put up his hands in horror and declined. No need to ask him what he thought of the Ashram. They slept in bunk beds which you made up yourself-having collected your sheets and bed clothes from the stores. A friend of Felicity's who is from Sligo had told her about this ashram and had spent a lot of time in it, ending up living in it full time. Not exactly the life we would wish for our children.
There were people of all nationalities there. You were called at 6 30am and went down to the local lake to meditate by sitting on a stone and crossing your arms while remaining silent. The ashram had a swimming pool where you had to be fully clothed to be allowed into it. Food was basic, no choice and tasted grand. There was an air of relaxation about the place and a sense of calm sadly lacking outside the gates. It would remind you of the kibbutz in Israel.

They had an introduction to one of the old colonial clubs from a former member now living in Ireland and were warmly greeted and were about to embark on a tour of the building when their guide saw Arun with them He was immediately asked to leave as it appears he was of a lower caste and no native Indians were allowed in whereupon Felicity and friends also walked out amazed that such separation still existed.
Later they took a boat on Lake Trivandrum for a two nights stay, famous for its silk. The food was top class as was the company and the staff. Local fishermen would come alongside the boat and you could buy lobsters from him or other fish including shellfish which they would cook for you on the boat. After that, they travelled down to Tiger Eager

country where the baboons would relieve you of anything not fully secured. The baboons were particularly partial to cameras.

A train journey was fitted in travelling in the public carriages a tight fit as ever you had with no room either to move or get food of any sort. Felicity had a bad sense of smell resulting from a fall down the steps in grannies as a child which in this situation was a blessing in disguise.

On reaching their destination in the far south they chanced a restaurant where the locals were eating out of aluminium basins with their hands, this proved too much for Felicity as the waiters who were all men stood looking at you after they placed the basin before you and all of them had big gaps in their yellow teeth as they grinned at you. After that, It was down in Trekked that Felicity got a phone call to tell her that her husband needed stenting and was being sent to Dublin immediately. It was a worrying time with her so far away, but all was well in the end. They ended their holiday in India at Bibi Baskins boutique hotel in Alleppey which was 70 euros per night and run by Bibi Baskin herself. She was away when they arrived but later appeared back from a wedding and was gasping for a gin and tonic as it was a wedding with no alcohol. Felicity was delighted to meet a fellow famous Irish woman as she was a well-known reporter on radio and television prior to going to India and she looked so elegant in her Indian garb worn to the wedding. Her boutique hotel is on a lovely beach and it is a famous place for flying kites. They all agreed that India was wonderful and would be on the agenda again for future years. The smiling faces and the eagerness of the people to make contact lent a warmth to the trip. Add to this the colourful saris, the whiteness of the men's shirts and their dark hair.The dense population, the poverty, the traffic and the potholes and yet the smiling faces. Arun was a gem never to be forgotten and Felicity kept up contact for many years.

They followed India the next year with Burma now known as Myanmar, then Sri Lanka, Brazil, Central America, specifically Guatemala, Nicaragua, Panama, Colombia, Vietnam and Cambodia, and this year its Equator and the Galapagos Islands. The same crew go every year but one of the women has three children in Australia and can't do both otherwise there would be five of them.

BURMA (Myanmar) was was a great experience tinged with sadness when you realise that some years later the Rohingya Muslims were driven out of their homes especially in Began the city of temples due to the military regime taking over and they had to flee Burma while the West failed to rally to their cause. It was Dublin—London-- Kuala Lumpur--into Yangon. As usual Felicity and co. would grab a day or two extras to explore before joining the group. It was Brids birthday and they found a famous old colonial hotel built by the Brits called the Old Strand Hotel, a Victorian relic which was the last word in portraying the architecture of the time. It had all the trimmings of footmen and amazing cocktails with cool air circulating to cool the heated brows.

Later that weekend they joined their travel group and their guide Su Mon, age 23, was serene and smiley. There was a small number in the travel group, only six and only two men. Felicity made a joke that they would have to share the two men, but they quickly declared that they were a happily married couple called Simon and Antonio with a colourful past. Simon had been a seminarian for several years, then left and got married and later separated, while Antonio was also married and had a 23-year-old daughter and was separated. They had met each other 3 years ago, got married and were now very happy. They were kind and helpful but rather critical of some of the odd habits of the Irish like drinking out of each other's bottles when thirsty.

It is a country of gentle people, very superstitious e g it is unlucky to cut your hair on Monday or Friday or on your birthday. It has 135 ethnic tribes the biggest being the Barma which make up 68% of the population. British rule brought roads, mines, and tea and coffee plantations with improved infrastructure especially roads and left behind colonial-era mansions. Yangon is the capital and houses the Sheraton Pagoda which dominates the whole city with its splendour. It is covered with sixty tons of pure gold and is one of the world's most spectacular religious monuments. Queen Shinsapu is supposed to have donated her weight in gold to this pagoda that she established. The most famous of the temples is the Andanmda temple dating back to 1094, in fact, they are spoilt for amazing temples in the heritage town of Began where there are 3000 Buddhist Temples.

A volcanic mountain was visited called Popa dates back to 443 BC when it first appeared after an earthquake. Here they visited the Mount Popa resort and were able to swim in their fabulous pool. Next, it was up the Ayeyarwady river to Mandalay and it was a bonus to see the sunrise over the Himalayas. The accommodation was at the Silver Star Hotel and it was only a short walk to the Teak Monastery and on to the Kandangyi Gardens.

Next on their agenda was Inlay Lake outside Began where the In-cha people live mainly in stilted houses over the lake. The area is known for its hot springs and massages, Floating gardens, leg rowers and island market., Burmese cats and lotus silks were some of the highlights. The leg rowers are unique to this area which involves standing on one foot in the boat with the other leg wrapped around the oar, as they row, it gets you there but looks weird. They ended their trip with a visit to the zoo, a well-run institution.

On their visit to Kolaw a town high up in the hills, they stayed in the Winner Hotel. That night they dined out in a restaurant called the 7 sisters. It transpired that it belonged to seven sisters whose father had been Irish. He was stationed in Myanmar during the war and met his future wife there. They had 7 girls and they were now running the restaurant. The food was lovely, but Felicity had to use the bathroom during the meal. This was only accessible via the basement and across the yard. On her way, she came across a young boy around 8 years of age washing the plates in a filthy slow-moving stream on his hunkers. Felicity was glad that none of the others were witness to this and did not say a word when she got back. No need to provoke sickness from thought rather than from reality and spoil the banana-parcelled fish which was delicious. One could always rely on the good old Ciproxin to kill all the toxins.

When you think about it Myanmar is the same size as France with a population of 60 million. Ninety per cent are Buddhists who lead a very simple life, hard to equate with the torture shed on the Rohingya Muslims driving them out of their country. Their president is Aung San Suu Kyi who spent years under house arrest and is pro-democracy, but it is a country where there is a constant struggle between hardliners and moderates within the government which shows no sign of moderating, the true rulers being the military. It looks as if Suu Kyi is being out manoeuvred by a government that has no intention of letting go of power. Leaving this exotic land behind, the awe-inspiring religious monuments of Yangon, its royal palace and stupa-filled planes of Began and heavenly Inlay lake and evocative Mandalay whose name is steeped in romance was like emerging from a dream. There was a consensus that it would be hard to beat Myanmar as a venue.

In 2015 it was back to Central America namely Brazil which started with a 7 am flight to Madrid only to be told that the flight was cancelled on arrival at the airport. This resulted in a compensation of 400 euros plus a flight to London and put up at a hotel overnight for their flight to Madrid the next day and on to Rio, a twelve-hour flight. Felicity said it was one great start to their holiday and wished it would happen more often. Rio Copacabana beach was on their doorstep with its super Flamingo music due to the central location of their hotel. It is not a beach for swimming as it is too polluted and there are pickpockets everywhere. They sat at the top of the beach enjoying the cocoa-nut drinks and people-watching.

They had a view of Christ The Redeemer out of their window which is a cross with Christ on top of Corcovado Mountain in praise of Jesus Christ erected in 1859. The structure is 30 metres high 709 metres above sea level A fantastic view could be obtained from the sugar loaf approached by a cable car made twice as good if it was sundown. They visited the Rio Maracand football stadium which seats 80 thousand in the open-air arena, refurbished in 2014 for the world cup. Alcohol had been banned in the stadium in 2003 but F.I.F.A got it back in 2014.

Another highlight was Sao Sebastian Cathedral famous for its stained glass windows which are stunning. On they went to Carnival Avenue with its array of shops where you could get your samba dress. They were duly ordered collected but ended up as nightwear as you would not be seen dead in them otherwise. Doreen did try to get an elegant dress made with better material but the result left a lot to be desired and she also was reduced to using it as a nightdress where even there it was a passion killer.

Their C E O tour guide was Ben, a good-looking long-haired hunk of 28 with smiling eyes and bare feet with dreadlocks and who was really cued into looking after his slightly older charges. He was 6 feet plus beside 5-foot Felicity. He fulfilled the bill. It was then on to Bonito and a go at white water rafting which nearly was the death of them as some of the rapids had 20 ft drops and a far cry from Felicity's previous experience of rafting in France which bore no resemblance to Brazil and it will be an experience she will not forget in a hurry.

The next visit was to Parity and The Iguacu National Park created in 1939 and containing jaguar, puma, caiman, and a collection of exotic birds now declared a world heritage site by UNESCO in 1986. The park is shared with Argentina and has the Iguazu falls in it These falls were viewed from the Brazilian side via a boat and all got soaked in the process but it was worth the discomfort as they were spectacular. It was on then to Paraty with its white buildings and cobblestone streets where once there were gold mines now replaced by tourists. They visited Bahia where they learned about the Bole Folkloric da Bahia folklore dance company, one of the 100 best in the world. They enjoyed a folklore concert that night and each evening the square resounded to live music in the evenings. The beaches were remote and underutilised but sea turtles resided there to add to the magic.

A highlight of the trip was The Pantanal in the wetlands of Brazil, an area the size of Europe. Transported there on the back of an open truck and sleeping in hammocks. On the side of the truck was a written age 18—35. Luckily the amigos were still colouring their hair and found themselves being admired as mother figures and wise old owls. They were met by their hosts and a swarm of mosquitoes and learned that in 2000 floods had wreaked havoc on the local farms washing away many of their cattle. You were surrounded by pigs, wild boar, herons, monkeys, storks, wild pheasants and birds of prey. You had to go down through a field to get to a toilet no mean feat in the middle of the night where you would be observed by fat frogs their bellies going in and out while you performed, When you flushed the toilet a scatter of small black frogs would come down with the water. On your journey back to the dorm if you looked to your right you could see the bright eyes of alligators watching you from the lake. It all elevated peeing to another level.

There was a fishing trip organised to the local lake much to Felicity's delight as it is her main hobby and she duly caught four piranhas while keeping a close eye on two alligators who were observing them from the lake. No way would the guides let her take the piranhas off the hook as they were known for their bite. Horse riding was on the agenda and Doreen's horse was stung with a bee and he bolted but she clung on for dear life. The Pantanal left a lasting impression and next it was San Salvador a city of culture duly explored and then it was on to San Paulo.

Now one of the group namely Brid who was much more religious than the other three was well in with the missionary priests and knew a local priest Fr Mc Gettrick who was stationed in Sao Paulo and had contacted him about the trip and assured the group that he said they were welcomed to come and stay with them but Father Mc Gettrick was only expecting one. They were duly met at the airport by Fr Mc Gettrick and it was later reported that first he saw one Irish emerge then two then three then four and wondered where they would put everyone, it was quite an invasion into a household of middle-aged plus men and in retrospect must have caused much scratching of hair and shaking of heads.
They were treated with kindness and care and it was one of the highlights of their trip. Felicity went shopping with Fr Mc Gettrick and did not spare the groceries she bought except that her card would not work when they got to the checkout and Father had to pay so embarrassingly. They were treated to great tales and stories by the priests, some of whom were there for over thirty years. They were also shown around the area and they treated the priests to a great night out before departing for home. They kept up contact with two of the priests back in Ireland.

The next year it was on to Sri Lanka previously known as Ceylon and known as the isle of contrasts including wildlife, cultural delights, tea plantations. and golden sands. As usual, they did their own thing after flying to Colombo via Dubai for the first few days.

They hired a driver with a car to show them the sights of Colombo. The Gangaramaya Buddhist temple, the clock tower lighthouse, the port and the new port being constructed by the Chinese and visiting the Dambulla National Park which has the largest number of wild elephants in the world. Travelling in jeeps to the river's edge where the elephants came to drink and get up really close to them was a really great experience. Felicity noticed that the elephants were being followed by white stork-like birds and was told that this was because the birds liked to explore the faeces of the elephants and get what they like out of them every man to his own.? One of the elephants had a baby and it was lovely to see how the herd protected him.

Sri Lanka is a Buddhist country where there are ancient statues, rock carvings, gilded temples, tea plantations and a tropical coastline. They met their group in Negombo and Sam was their guide, another gem, G adventures seem to have a knack for getting super guides. The group were a mixture of Canadians, English, Germans, Koreans and of course the four elderly Irish. A trip on the Dutch Canal to view the wild bird life and see the fishermen drying their fish on the sands was taken. Here you could also go whale watching. They also went to the Gally national park to search for leopards, another world heritage site. The Dutch ruled here for many years.

Next on their agenda was Dambulla where they saw the Buddhist cave temples filled with Buddhist statues and heard the tale of a tourist that sat on top of one of them and broke the buddha, a crime of major proportions. Felicity excused herself from visiting the fortress of Sigiriya, a world heritage site involving 1200 steps but when you are on the wrong side of 66 you must forgo some cultural experiences.
They did have the opportunity to see the Royal Botanical gardens and the house where Lord Louis Mountbatten was stationed during the war

and where his wife and the wife of Nehen the president of India were reputed to swap partners; I suppose to relieve the boredom.
No trip to Sri Lanka would be complete without seeing Kandy and the temple of the tooth, the spice plantations, the alligators, and especially the exotic birds.

A home visit was organised with a cookery demonstration. They were taught how to plate coconut fronds to make thatch for roofs. The shell of the coconut is used for cups and later as fuel, It is also used to make door mats, coconut oil, meal flour milk and is used in cosmetics so nothing in the coconut goes to waste.

They had the experience of travelling by train to the Gurdwara plains, second class standing part of the trip and were exposed to the monsoon rains. They saw Richmond house owned by Queen Mary and King George the 5th now a school for the underprivileged. It was an activity-packed holiday with something for everyone. They ended their trip with a few relaxing days in the seaside city of Negombo. After Sri Lanka the next on the list was Colombia.

It was with great excitement that they set off for Colombia in 2015 doing the initial 2 to 3 days on their own before joining up with the others on the tour. This emerging country with a resurgence of culture, art and the Latin-Caribbean fusion of colours and flavours. A country plagued by drug barons and crime up until now. A land of cocaine barons, guerrillas and emerald mines, invaded by the Spanish in 1499 and they established the first town Santa Marta in 1525 followed by Cartagena in 1533. Now a country of over 89 million people with 2 coasts the Caribbean and the Pacific housing 90 per cent of the population Bogota founded in 1538 is now the capital.

Their flight was to Bogotá via Madrid. They hired a driver called Hector to show them the sights of Bogotá which he did and brought them to the equator crossing outside Bogotá. A decisive battle was fought for independence led by Bolivar in 1819 which was successful but was followed by eight years of civil wars at which time the U.S.A took advantage of the country's strife and moved in to create a republic which included Panama and they opened the Panama Canal which remained under dispute until 1921.

Civil war raged on, fought by guerrillas, the most notorious of these groups known as the FARC. Thousands of people died even after the liberals and the conservatives united to try to rule the country. The Farc are no longer supported by Moscow or Havana and are financed by robbing, extortion, kidnapping and the drug trade. Colombia produces 80% of the World's cocaine production and in the early 1980s, the drug trade was led by Pablo Escobar. This continued until 1993 until eventually Pablo was killed.

Life was never dull for these four, on their first morning while eating breakfast on the 8th floor they got a funny smell of burning which got worse by the minute so that people were suddenly wearing masks, then someone said there was a case on fire in one of the bedrooms but that they had got it under control and now had the case out on the balcony. Felicity and co. wandered out to the balcony to see the offending article and there was this case well burned and its contents destroyed. Felicity remarked that it was like her case and that someone must have had the same case as her. It was quite a while before it sunk in that it was Felicity's case when she eventually recognized some of the burned clothes. The bedrooms in the hotel in Columbia all had cookers and were very small so Felicity had pushed her case over on the cooker to make room and must have turned on a knob in the process. Luckily, she had her documentation out of the case and her shoes but everything else was destroyed.

The upshot of this was several trips to shops to replace essentials aided by her good friends loaning knickers, pyjamas, socks and whatever else they could spare. She ended up getting some very nice bits and marvelling at how little you really need. The staff were incredibly helpful but were adamant that the police should not be called,something Felicity thought would get her a report that would enable her to have an insurance claim. In fact if you think about it Felicity was at fault ,the room was destroyed, there was smoke damage and a European country might have landed her with a substantial bill added to the fact that they were not due to join the tour group until that evening.

Hector showed them all the sights of Bogota including the Salt Cathedral outside Bogota in Zipaquira built in the 6th century and a church beside it built in 1950. The 470-year-old historic city centre is awash with cafes, guest houses, and historic sites known as La Candelabra. Food is quite spicy, and the portions are huge, so they requested a doggie bag which caused much discussion. They passed the doggie bag on to Hector and later heard him telling the hotel staff the story to gales of laughter.

The Andes runs down the western coast with the Sierra Nevada across the north sheltering Santa Marta. It is the highest coastal mountain range in the world boarding both the Pacific and the Caribbean.

Spain's strong Catholic traditions left behind many spectacular churches and convents.The best example of pre-Columbian urban planning can be seen in the Lost City adjacent to Santa Martha built by the Indians consisting of a network of terraces, paths and stairways.

Columbia is 5 hours behind us in time, its music is predominately African with the coastal areas preferring the Spanish Rhythm. Its museums ,shanty towns, historic quarter, and the Plaza de Bolivar lend a mystique to its surroundings. It is estimated that one quarter of fake U S dollars circulating worldwide are made in Columbia.

Felicity's group bought the well-known book by Garcia Marquez, One Hundred Years of Solitude which won the Nobel prize for literature in 1982 and was interesting reading while visiting Columbia. In 1999 Columbia was struck with an earthquake leaving 250 thousand homeless and two thousand dead. Bogota proved to be a fascinating city and under Hector's guidance they saw the splendid colonial churches. It is now a city of over seven million people.

It was on next to Cerro de Monserrat to catch the funicular to the top of the mountain and what a view and so well explained by Hector. It was here in Bogotá that they joined the rest of the group from Cornwell, Dundee, Canada, Amsterdam, London, Minneapolis and Iran. Their guide's name was Louis. A flight the next day to Arimina re named by the inhabitants to remember the genocide of Armenians by Turks to visit a coffee plantation. Here they learned not to buy the dark brown coffee bean as it is probably burned and is very sharp to taste. There was singing, dancing and fancy dress at the plantation. They visited the gold museum and Doreen won at a game of Tejo. Nine hours' drive by bus over the Andes to Medellin, once the most dangerous city in the world now revamped and its streets are safe again with easy access to most parts of the city. This was achieved by forming vigilantes' groups and giving them permission to shoot on site anyone stealing, fighting or partaking in any crime, so we now have a big turnabout since its notorious days as the Centre of Colombia's drug trade. It does have its own unique character added to by the fabulous graffiti unique in its artistic beauty. Neighbourhoods are infused with winding streets and much greenery. A cable car extension of the subway connects the low income barrios to the centre.

Everyone has heard of Pablo Escobar, probably the most famous drug baron that ever lived who on one hand gave to the poor while wreaking havoc on the drug scene. They visited his prison where he eventually landed after demanding to have the prison built for him to his specifications including a swimming pool, golf course , gym e t c and then succeeded in bribing all the security guards so that he was able to easily escape when he wanted to. They got a tour around this so-called prison which is now an old people's home and inhabited by the doting, the incapacitated and the very old who enjoy great views, fresh air, and the surroundings. Pablo would buy a block of apartments such as the La Monico block in Medellin for poor people to live in. He was betrayed by the Cali Cartel and shot in 1993 at the age of 43 after being on the run for four hundred and ninety nine days. They visited his grave which is a very modest grave for someone so famous. Medellin is on the side of a hill and they have built escalators that make it a pleasure to explore this town.

On to the romantic aura of Cartagena and we changed guides to Philippe. Cartagena is a city of fairy tale romance, legends and sheer beauty with cobbled alleys, balconies, bougainvillaea and massive churches. It is the main Spanish port on the Caribbean coast with elaborate walls encircling it. Here they had the experience of having dinner in the women's prison served by the inmates. Felicity was amazed at the female prisoners who were so young and many of them were beautiful-looking girls. The meal was superb and the ambience was convivial. They visited Castillo San Felipe and travelled by horse-drawn carriages. The accommodation was in a hostel 20 minutes from the beach.

Felicity got lost in the woodland on the way back from the beach and they organised a search party to go out to look for her led by Eric from Dundee. A secluded wooded area was not the safest place to get lost. Cartagena with its colonial walls and fortress was followed by a break in Santa Martha where you can listen to the hummingbirds in the trees. Here is where the Colombians holiday as it offers long stretches of sandy beaches with hotels, casinos and many man-made attractions. This is where they visited the aquarium, the National park, the gold museum and the Cathedral and many other attractions.
Felicity had met a neighbour before coming to Columbia who told her to look up a friend in Santa Marta, an architect, who was now running a hostel there. They eventually found the hostel, but the friend was not there, however, they knew they were in the right place as the wi-fi password was written in Irish pog mo thoin translated kiss my ass.

On to Crystal Island and Dead man's bay. Felicity who was mad to get fishing got her wish and was joined by Mark, a 30-year-old from the group. When they went to the boat it was a dugout canoe. Where am I expected to go to the toilet? says Felicity and was told there is a bucket in the boat. The sea was very rough and Felicity, who knew the sea was not very happy so the crew put them on a deserted beach, with plenty of rocks there to go behind. Felicity was thrilled to catch a big tuna which she brought to the restaurant. They cooked it, and everyone got a bite as their starter, but she was sorry that Mark had not caught it as he was new to fishing.

Santa Martha is the oldest surviving city in South America. It is where Simon Bolivar lived and died, his heart is buried in Santa Martha and his body in Caracas. Columbia left a lasting impression on the amigos, how they had gotten on top of corruption and crime but still unfortunately had a serious drug problem. Felicities group were telling the younger members how they had never been offered drugs since coming to

Columbia but learned that the younger members had been approached nearly every day with offers, thank god for grey hair.

Their next port of call was to be Vietnam and Cambodia the following year. Off went the four to Vietnam first. Here the hordes of people are what strikes you. The absence of streetlights for crossing the roads so you take your life in your hands, put out your foot and pray you get to the other side and miraculously you do. The first time is the worst and then it becomes normal after a short time. People watching became a fascinating pastime, whole families on push bicycles, father and child in front, mother behind with another child in between wedged between mother and father left to negotiate the chaotic traffic. Over and above this is the constant noise and never did Felicity see an accident during all this time.

They were a gentle, loving people and so helpful, quaint and hospitable. This is despite their brutal past being occupied first by the Chinese then the French and laterally by the Americans. These have all left a rich cultural footprint as well as a brutal imprint, but the Vietnamese amazingly hold no recriminations. It was a land of craggy limestone formations, mountains, jungles, river deltas and pristine beaches. They flew into Hanoi and per usual their hotel was very central and three stars. Hanoi is the capital with a population of over 3.5 million people. They enjoyed the old quarter and explored the museum of fine arts and the mausoleum. It was an overnight train then to Sapa and Loi Chai to visit the minority tribes. of which there are 54 in existence.

The visit to Halong Bay where the towering rock formations made of limestone rise majestically out of the ocean was spectacular. It boasts 3000 islands of towering limestone. The amigos were also able to enjoy some kayaking and swimming as well as the spires and coves. Next, it was on to the central coast and Hue, a former Vietnam capital. In Hue, they saw the walled Citadel and the Imperial City plus the Tombs of the Nguyen Emperors. The perfume river with its dragon boats, houseboats and long tail boats selling a variety of goods including many beautiful varieties of flowers, crafts etc.

Ho Chi Minh City, previously known as Saigon, is chaotic with over 7 million people. Here they visited the Vietnam History museum depicting their long struggle against the French, the Chinese and the Americans. Evidence of the country's past wars can be seen in the tunnels of Vinh Moc near Hue and the hideouts in the Mekong Delta, famous for its rice production.

Felicity would say that the evocative war memorials gave a sad reminder of the suffering these people endured due to the wars with America and France and how it applied in equal measures to Cambodia as well as to Vietnam. Despite this, these people have put conflicts and occupation behind them and have remained quaint and hospital as well as friendly. A further picture is portrayed by visiting the demilitarised zone D M2 where you see the underground tunnels which Felicity was able to get into as she was small like the Vietnamese. These were escape routes for the Vietnamese who are small people and could get through them whereas the larger Americans could not. Their ingenuity in fighting the war was so impressive and so brutal. These resistant fighters dug holes and lowered spikes into them, then covered them with grass and their opponents would step on them and get impaled on the spikes, so tragic for both sides in an unnecessary war.

In Cambodia, they flew to Siem Reap to see the fabulous Angkor Wat Temple complex which once between the 13th and 15th century formed the centre of the mighty Khmer Empire. The dozens of temple complexes of Anger Wat are best seen at sunrise. This is one of Asia's most enchanting destinations. The best time to visit to get a cloud-free sunrise is between November and March.

Vietnamese communists' outposts in Cambodia drew it into the Vietnam conflict and Cambodia was bombed by American forces in the late 1960s. A military coup followed in 1970 but in 1975 the infamous Khmer Rouge led by Pol Pot took over Cambodia. Opposition was brutally crushed resulting in the death of over two million Cambodians. Pol Pot died in 1998 and a truce was eventually established by the United Nations.

Felicity found the killing fields of Cambodia and the Tuol Sleng Prison devastating in its cruelty where men, women and children were interned during the Khmer Rouge regime from 1975--- to 1979 during which Cambodians were driven from their homes subjected to brainwashing, forced into labour camps and many were executed   Note how recently all this happened when Cambodia was drawn into the Vietnamese war after the 1960 troubles started.

The Khmer Empire ruled from the 10th to the 15th century. Trouble began at the end of 1960 when the communists were using Cambodia to wage war on Vietnam and it was then that America entered the war against the communists, a situation that continued until March 70. It is estimated that between one and two million people died of starvation, disease, overwork, or execution during the Kumar Rouge genocide. The people worst affected were the teachers, professionals, doctors, skilled workers, monks and artists etc. The Kumar Rouge exploited the corruption of the government and recruited youth to join their cause. Eventually they became so powerful they invaded Cambodia and forced huge numbers of them to live in labour camps and work 14 to 18 hours a day. They tortured and killed innocent people including babies and mothers and starved many of them to death. This was all portrayed in the Killing Fields of Cambodia and it would make you weep. The rulers at this time were led by Pol Pot and his extended family which consisted of about 79 people. Felicity had no problem in naming this trip as the saddest trip ever and its everlasting effect on one's inability to understand man's inhumanity to man in the modern age and that no one tried to help. Cambodia became and still is one of the world's poorest nations. It is now becoming a favourite tourist attraction and is experiencing a 5% annual growth.

They visited the capital Phnom Penh saw the Sisowath Quay on the riverfront, the Silver Pagoda, and the National Museum and the Museum of Genocide compounding the history already seen and heard.

Felicity's last trip was to Central America including Guatemala. Nicaragua and Panama and luck was on their side as Doreen, one of the group had a timeshare in Guatemala, so they were able to live in luxury for one week. It is a fascinating country with its wealth of volcanoes, isolated Mayan remains and stunning cloud forests. Guatemala is noted for its Mayan textiles. 60 per cent of the population are Mayas and there are 20 separate languages. On the political front, it is a country of corruption, violence and injustice. As might be expected there are magnificent Mayan ruins, world-class markets, and rumbling volcanoes but a violent crime rate.

Felicity would say it was the country where they were most afraid and never stayed out after 9 o'clock. It is interesting that one night in a restaurant finishing at 8 o'clock they were going to walk home but the boss literally forbade them and insisted they take a taxi. They explored the lush Rio Dulce by boat and had endless fun bargaining at the many markets.

Next, it was on to Nicaragua with its well-preserved colonial cities all cheap and cheerful. With the demise of support from the U.S.S.R. in 1989 and the election of Violette Charro, the U.S. trade embargo was lifted, and the country started on the road to recovery and stability. It is the biggest country in Central America. Nicaragua is a country that has been hit by violence in the 20th century. The population is 5.5 million and it has been dogged by repeated volcanoes and flooding. Their economy is the second worst in Central America, but it is considered today to be one of the safest countries in Central America having survived dictatorships, revolutions, civil war and economic collapse. Felicity found that dollars stretched far here and that they were a kind, proud people. This country is famous of course for the ancient lands of the Maya in Conan and other cities with their seductive colonial settings such as the Cathedral in Granada. It also is the least densely populated country in Central America.

Next, it was to see some of the active and dormant volcanoes with beach time in San Juan Del Sur or Rockton and what about the nature lover's paradise on Ometepe Ish2gland. They ate with a family there on the biggest lake in Central America.

After Nicaragua, she moved on to Panama a country where you can explore cloud forests, snortle the Caribbean and visit the coffee plantations but of course, it is most famous for being the passageway for the large ships from Australia, New Zealand heading for Europe a trade that makes over 4 million U S dollars a day. Felicity and her companions were lucky enough to book a passage through the canal which is very spectacular and of historical significance. Its 80 km belt of locks which brings the Atlantic to the Pacific, wedding East to West. Monster freighters and Capuchin monkeys share the canal. It was possible to get a hop-on hop-off bus in Panama and the group found these buses a great way to get acquainted with a city and you could go back to interesting parts. The evidence of wealth was everywhere, and Panama is well known as a safe haven for hot money. Certainly, there was plenty to add to one's knowledge of culture, enjoyment and appreciation in their Central America trip.

They were off again. Flights from Dublin to Paris, overnight in Paris, Paris to Atlanta and the dreaded customs that are as rude as predicted. A further thirteen hours to Quito. This was one journey that they found very challenging and wondered if their far-flung trips might be coming to an end.

Quito is 2800 feet above sea level. A great city with its hop-on hop-off bus and its cable car called the Telefonica up Vulcan Pichincha to the top giving spectacular views over Quito and the Andes which surround it like a spinal column running down the middle. Its museums, spas, music and monasteries, its Spanish colonial architecture and many other gems added to by the local exotic colours make it a natural and cultural wonder. At 12 million population, many of Indian extraction it is the most densely populated country in South America.

As was their modus operandi they arrived 3 days ahead of their organised group. Again as occurs with all the G Adventure itineraries their 2-star hotels were both central within walking distance of Plaza de la Independence the main hub of Quito. As Quito sits on the equator it gives a chance to stand with one foot in each hemisphere at the middle of the world. Later in Quito, they joined a particularly nice group from G adventures. There were two guides, one for Ecuador and one for the Galapagos and they were both excellent. It was off to the Galapagos the next morning which is 1000 km from Quito, formed by a series of eruptions below the surface of the ocean millions of years ago.

The islands are amazing, sea lions with pups lying all over the place on piers, sands and rocks, living in harmony with iguanas, the only place in the world where the iguanas can swim are called marine iguanas. Add to this turtles, manta rays, red and blue boobies, no they are not boobies as we know them, they are a species of birds, pelicans a bird persons paradise, we must not forget the tortoises which have been protected and nurtured in special compounds if sick or injured.

The islands played a key role in confirming Darwin's theory of evolution from single-cell organisms through fish, reptiles, birds, and eventually mammals through survival of the fittest. After he had spent time studying the unique species on the island he was able to better understand his theory of evolution.

They visited 3 islands in the Galapagos, Santa Cruz the most developed, Isabella the largest and Floriana which has only 150 people. The people here were financed by G adventures to improve their houses to do home stays and each night one house will feed the visitors. It is a brilliant idea to give these people a source of income and impressive to find a travel business taking such an interest in people and the environment.

Felicity said it was not necessary to even try to explain the attractions of their beaches, waterfalls, forests, the clean clear water for swimming and snorkelling On a lighter note Felicity mentioned the spas and many natural hot springs which were present outside every bedroom in one lodge they stayed in and at one spa you ordered your cocktail on entry and it arrived on a small boat across the pool, once in a lifetime. In Santa Cruz, they ate street food. This meant one street was cleared of traffic and tables were put down in the centre of the street. The catering was done from both sides of the street and there were the most delicious fish of all sorts to choose from. Fish lovers rave about ceviche, a raw fish marinated in lemon juice flavoured with onion and chilli and served with popcorn. Travelling between the islands was by speed boats; Soup was served with almost every meal and the variety was delicious.

After the islands, it was back to Ecuador and Quito. Both Mary and Doreen got sick around this time with a bad cough, a temperature and breathlessness. Luckily Felicity had antibiotics with her and steroids and they were started on treatment but the improvement was slow and Doreen started looking up flights to fly home. This would have cost 600 pounds more and Mary, also a medic, thought she might be in heart failure. Slowly they emerged from this and in retrospect, one would wonder if it might be coved19 as it had started at that time with a vengeance in China. Felicity noted that she had entered in her diary that a potent virus was sweeping across China not realising that it was going to take over the world.

Climbers are drawn to this country to climb Cotopaxi which is outside the town of Banos. Cotopaxi is the highest active volcano in the world at 5900 metres. Sleeping in one of the lodges in the Andes they were appreciative of a fire in the bedroom and a hot water bottle in the bed. The following day it was the train passage through the Andes which commenced building in 1806 by prisoners of war who would get a pardon if they worked on making the railway through the mountain. The train runs between Riobamba and Sibambe 3 days a week and takes in the hair-raising Devil's Nose. The country's railway pride and joy but with a sad history. Of the prisoners of war who worked on the railway come hail or snow to get the railway completed 2000 of them died in the effort which finished in 1965. Now it is to entertain visitors. You would not be human if you were not tinged with sadness at the history of this railway. Started in 1806 and was overseen by foremen who were merciless their only aim was to fulfil the instructions of the military working under conditions that included no machinery, blunt chisels, scorching sun, and poor nutrition. Limited supplies of axes and saws to clear the jungle and not enough stones to re-sharpen their tools if you could call them tools. The men were beaten if they fell behind and were called lazy. One of the problems referred to was the prisoners running away or dying. Cholera was often a welcome killer in an impossible situation. They were considered less than men, just material to make the railway like the teak sleepers, the steel rails or the dog spikes. They were often given a week's rations and expected to work for a month. The suffering was unimaginable. It was with a heavy heart that the group came back to base.

Felicity and her friends found it a physically challenging trip and wondered what the future held but were already talking about the great continent of Africa but first, there was an invisible bombshell waiting to consume the world, the coronavirus or covid-19.

The next trip did not materialise for two and a half years due to covid virus taking over the world, and preventing travel between countries, restrictions placed by different countries and due to lockdown the farthest you could travel was five kilometres. Much cancelling for the previous two and a half years left a nice little nest egg to fall back on and vouchers were the only way not to lose your money

First, it was Cyprus direct from Dublin to Paphos and a 4-star hotel with her friend Brid. Many retired guests with their sticks and walkers there on a long-term basis and predominantly British, not surprising when you hear the history of Cyprus and the length of British rule. Felicity and her friend made their way to the bus station the next day and discovered that you could get a bus ticket daily that allowed you to travel extensively for the day and they gladly made full use of this offer. They made friends with 2 other ladies much younger who booked the spa for 5 30 each evening and joined them there, a friendship which lasted and ended up with their 2 friends coming to the Galway Races. Cyprus was very interesting historically and had a perfect climate in March. On one of their trips up north, they visited where the tourists were few and far between. There they had a problem getting a café opened and when they wanted to visit the marina no taxi was available however a gentleman at an adjoining table approached them and offered to drive. Felicity eyed him and decided that he looked frail, that Brid was strong and that she could kick if necessary and she gratefully accepted the offer. It turned out he had left Cyprus when he was 16, going to England and ended up in Saudi Arabia and had become very wealthy. He had got married when he was 50 and had 5 children and his problem now he told them was loneliness and he wasn't very well as he had kidney cancer. They invited him down to dinner in Papos and kept in contact with him after coming back to Ireland. A highlight of this trip was the friendships they made, how the guests would gather around in the evening to enquire where they had been and another couple who lived near Felicity's daughter was able to recommend a builder as they were having problems getting one. It was a very positive experience.

Felicity and another friend of hers Mary Flood had booked a trip to the Artic on the cruise ship Hurtigruten from Bergen in Norway twice cancelled due to covid and the excitement was high. Disaster struck the day before going when her friend came down with covid and couldn't go. The big question now was would Felicity go on her own? Never one to pass a challenge she decided to chance it. It was pre-arranged to meet five colleagues in Dublin the day before in Nollaigs house and a great day was had after which Felicity made her way to the Maldrone Hotel for an overnight and off the next morning. Her travelling companion struggled up to the airport to give her the tickets. A friend who had a daughter in Oslo gave her her number and instructions on how to get to central Oslo from the airport. On reaching Oslo she was aware that the hotel was nearby, supposed to be within a five-minute walk so she saw a man in a uniform relaxing outside the station and approached him to inquire about the hotel. He consulted google and said he would walk her to the hotel, a polish guy, so helpful, and he left her at the door.
There were 2 days booked in Oslo which is a very beautiful city and by using the hop-on hop-off bus she saw all the sights including the opera house.

The next day it was a super train journey over the mountains from Oslo to Bergen lasting six hours and is a famous journey of forests, mountains and snowscapes. As time in Bergen was limited it was straight to the hotel and off to the cruise ship the following day. Felicity noted a lady on her own in the waiting room of the cruise ship and she took a seat near her. The lady turned around and asked her the time and Felicity asked her if she was travelling alone which she was and she asked Felicity if they could eat together at dinner, her name was Dianna Chamberlain and she was widely travelled and of similar age from Fort Lauderdale in Florida. It turned out to be a very interesting friendship as she was a theatre nurse, excellent at researching the terrain and reading maps. Their shared experiences, similar tastes in food and adventurous spirits meant they gelled well. The cabins were pathetic like a cubby hole with no window and it never got dark. Obviously, they were the cheaper cabins. As compensation, Felicity's cabin was beside the 2 jacuzzis on board and she loved lying in this elevated jacuzzi in the heat and watch the snow-capped mountains pass by. Although there were 300 on board, less than a dozen used the jacuzzi and it was a good venue to meet people. What was not explained about the cruise was that there were daily excursions from the boat all costing over 100 euros but necessary to get a full picture of the artic.

The boat was a delivery boat smaller than a regular cruise ship and able to go in and out of all the fjords making deliveries and collecting goods. While at port you could go into the little towns as you might have an hour and a half. Many of the excursions involved visiting islands, seeing old churches, and getting a view of the Viking way of life, including tea and pancakes. One trip which Felicity really enjoyed was the king crab excursion. They went in a rib boat after being laced up into a space-like suit and then travelled at great speed to lift the crab pots. King crabs came originally from Russia. They are a scavenger type crab, like the spider crab but 4 times the size . They are a scavenger type crab which feed on the bed of the ocean and reproduce at a great rate. They eat anything and everything and it is important that they are fished regularly to keep their numbers down. There were 14 on the excursion and they got 12 crabs which the boatman cooked in boiling water for half an hour with sea salt. They were served up with plain bread and every last bit was eaten and they were delicious.

They visited lighthouses, Viking villages, fisherman's homes, fishing tackle workshops, many churches and graveyards which were fascinating to see the names on the graves, very many of the same name showing the number of intermarriages. It was also a bonus that the cruise included the celebrations of the 19th of May, their big day like Patrick's day at home. At all the small ports that day they were met by music and bands. It's called independence day. On that day the captain came to the assembly on deck. Everyone was given a flag, the national anthem was sung and there was champagne and brandy and people volunteered to be baptised, meaning you had water poured down your neck. No polar bears were seen on the trip but there were many whales, orcas, dolphins and eagles. It was the wrong time of the year for the northern lights. It is notable though that it is bright practically all night ,something that escapes your notice in the cabins that have no window. It was the end of a trip of a lifetime landing back into Bergen where Felicity got a taxi to the airport for her flight back to Oslo where she had a night booked and was able to collect her stored goods.

Airports around this time became a nightmare as people were suddenly starting to travel post covid although covid was by no means gone but countries had relaxed the rules and people were on the move. You had to be at the airport 3 hours before the flight and even then people were missing their flights. Felicity flew Oslo Stansted and again due to Brexit it took almost an hour to get through customs where her son-in-law Mathew was waiting for her and she was never so glad to see anyone to relinquish her responsibilities to him. Felicity had one day with her daughter and then it was off to Lanzarote to a fab house booked two years previously but blocked by covid. It was a fab holiday with no responsibility, Mathew driving all over the island to fisherman's villages and remote spots well removed from the hustle and bustle. It was time to bond with the grandchildren, to swim, walk, climb, visit aqua parks, go kayaking and get a tan. Not bad going for a 78-year-old woman. Felicity was eternally grateful to have the health to do it all.

CHAPTER ELEVEN CORONA VIRUS
****

Felicity had the honour or horror of living through the on-slough of the coronavirus which started in China in January 2020, but China is a long way away and there are often odd occurrences there like the Tiananmen square massacres so there was scant heed paid to it when it first made its presence felt there. Initially, it was only an item on the news bulletin, there was an element of distance and criticism of China's inability to contain it. A very important lesson in being too self-righteous. It was a virus that can affect anyone and respects no one and quickly changed the World. Lucky for China they were a communist country with a dictator in place. Do as I say or die, thousands died. This is a virus that is stalking the world right now moving easily through the most stringent restrictions.

Corvid 19 is a new disease that often presents atypically in older patients and whose management is complex. While the majority present with a mild to moderate infection a small percentage progress to severe disease including viral pneumonia with multiple organ failure. Clotting problems may surface when you think recovery is in progress. It is a virus like no other its huge strength is its infectiousness, spreading like wildfire and thriving, with limited treatments available opening an avenue for quacks, healers and many others with tales of weird and wonderful cures never tested by regular scientific research like Chloroquine, a drug used against malaria and arthritis and shown to have been effective in a small cohort of covid 19 cases but later shown to be of little benefit. Felicity got her stash of Chloroquine and Zithromax, an antibiotic they were combining with it in case she got it. Her policy was as there was no treatment, so this was better than nothing even Donald Trump put himself on it as a preventive so she was in good company.

First, there were 5 cases then there were 12 and so on it went like a frog jumping from one pond to the other and infecting all before him. Italy was the first European country to be hit, a people who hug and kiss, emotional people. In no time at all, they were the most affected in

Europe closely followed by Spain. Borders were closed, plane flights cancelled leaving people stranded in foreign countries and on it went. Felicity and her pals were so lucky to get home before the shutdown started.

The old, the infirm, those with co-morbidity were in danger. The media, the papers, TV and Radio were non-stop broadcasting about it all day. The anxious and the mentally compromised became mental wrecks listening all day to news bulletins talking about self-isolation, talking about death and talking about the government. The emphasis shifted to damage limitation, prevention and containment.

Personal protective equipment was ordered in great quantities, hand washing became the norm in all public places, timely testing and obtaining results, contact tracing, social distancing was introduced. All over 70s had to cocoon in other words stay indoors.

It is amazing to compare it to previous pandemics like the outbreak in Germany in 1527 in which the German reformer Martin Luther said, we will not socialise, shall fumigate, help purify the air, administer the medicine, and take it. I will avoid places and persons where my presence is not needed in order not to become contaminated and thus by chance infect and pollute others and so cause their death as a result of my negligence. Very similar to the present advice. The media said that hospitals would be swamped. That only the young and the normally healthy would be treated as there was insufficient health care to deal with the old and the already sick. Intensive care beds were at a premium.

This led to acute anxiety among some including the children. One 13-year-old was crying because he got a temperature and a sore throat and thought he was going to die. Suicide shot up in the teens in England. Schools were closed and a 6 ft space was to be observed between people in public places, shopping, queues, or out walking.
All sports were cancelled including the Olympics. All social activities, dances, theatre, movies, concerts, were put on hold. Weddings were suspended or done with only a witness to be properly celebrated later. It

was nothing but gloom and doom and more gloom with predictions of a severe recession and poverty to follow. Countries went into lockdown. In G.P Surgeries administrative tasks were conducted by phone or video consultation, the aim being infection prevention.

The College put on twice weekly National web server updates with up to 900 G.Ps participating. It removed the ability to meet in person, new skills had to be learned, redeployments, altering their training, their assessment and their exams. The order of the day became video conferencing. They are missing the face-to-face meetings and their small group education but must get used to the new norm, that is what you signed up to when you become a doctor. There is a continual wheel of misinformation that the family doctor battles daily added to by research overload. For families that have relatives very ill or dying the inability to visit or indeed even talk to them by phone was a source of considerable distress and frustration. We are seeing and hearing of lonely deaths in isolation rooms which is deeply saddening.

Our only hope is the development of a vaccine or so many get it that eventually there will be herd immunity. Masks have proved to be controversial but the evidence from other countries is positive as a prevention. With all this cocooning there is a surge in cases of anxiety, depression, loneliness and a desperate need for support. The calls to helplines in the past 6 months have doubled and now stand at 30,973. Electronic medical records are being used to send prescriptions electronically, reducing transmission risk, to improve quality of care, patient outcome and safety. The commuter trains are almost empty, the sandwich and Susie chains are giving notice on their leases. Takeaway restaurants are doing a brisk business. People are working from home or zooming. Landlords are losing tenants as office blocks get emptied out. Restaurants and shops are empty. Transport networks are quiet.
What has it done to our children turned them into clingy terrified robots, Is it ok to go on the slide, can I go on the swing? Our children have become our shadows and they have lost the ability to be naughty.
After effects need to be recognised, called long covid which presents with extreme tiredness, mobility problems, loss of smell, functional swallowing, cognitive impairment and mental health issues occurring in

ten per cent of covid cases. In turn, other services such as physiotherapy, speech therapy, occupational therapy, podiatry, and psychological services are all cancelled or massively reduced.
So much has changed since the middle of March that the World seems scarcely recognisable. Wherever one goes there is the evidence of infection control and prevention. Plastic screens, face masks, hand gels, and floor markings are everywhere and a new normal has come into being. One woman wrote that she had dyed her hair pink and put on green nail varnish to go on another f---walk. These recommendations include community assessment hubs, an effective system of test and trace. Physical layout of practices, staff training, cleaning arrangements, adherence to standard precautions such as hand hygiene, cough etiquette and social distancing are critical. There is a need to make these top priority and standard items at all practice meetings.
Practice incomes have taken a hit and costs have risen. The chronic disease protocol for those over 70s is a welcome source of finance when implemented in the practice. Many consultations end up as one done by phone only to be repeated face to face doubling the workload while G.P.s find remote consultations by video link very tiring and unsatisfactory. Stress must be kept at bay by encouraging leisure activities, exercise, and family time.

It is a little-known disease but appears to attack the respiratory system, unfortunately sometimes progressing to multi-organ and systemic magnifications such as sepsis, shock and multi-organ dysfunction syndromes. Mortality rates remain between 1 and 2 per cent More cases are being reported with myocardial injury and dysfunction Renal involvement are also being reported.

Viruses were not discovered until 1930 when the electron microscope was invented and the first virus affecting humans was seen in 1948. Vaccines were discovered in 1796 due to an outbreak of smallpox although the outbreak of Spanish flu in 1918 which had a death toll of 50 million is the main pandemic against which pandemics are measured. At present Oxford appears to be the nearest to getting a vaccine against corvid 19 but if it will work and for how long only time will tell. Meanwhile, we struggle on in this new world.

Limitations were placed on the number of people attending funerals and people that were in contact with a case had to quarantine for 14 days. Thousands of people were out of work, many were not sure their job would survive the downturn. At higher financial levels shares fell, thousands of euros were wiped off the financial markets. Eventually, when the numbers had reached over the 1000-deaths there was almost a complete shutdown of all public services except services considered essential like supermarkets, hospitals etc.

Time for the oldies to get computer literate. They need to be able to order their groceries online to be delivered or have someone to do the shopping for them. It is amazing how the world adapts, are we creatures of habit or are we followers of fashion? Restaurants were something of the past but if you complained you were told people are dying. No cinema, no theatre. Another cartoon shows two dogs talking about humans and how they are all wearing mussels and that it must be because they had never learned to sit on command. If you did not comply you were stupid, selfish or ignorant and then the police were involved and were very active.

There was a wave also of love, thoughtfulness and kindness helping the cocooned. Visiting them, running messages for them, getting their prescriptions. People started to greet people and talk to them at 2 metres apart. If you work from home a big house will give you the space to have an office of your own. Despite the disconcerting circumstances it is possible to enjoy the slower pace of life, listen to the birds singing, to admire the garden and the flowers, to study the sky and the stars and make time for others. To go back to nature, to slow down but not so much that you become horizontal.

Leo Varadkar excelled himself in his management and reporting on it, in implementing the rules and regulations around exposure to it. He also dealt with the economic fallout, people losing their jobs, businesses going to the wall, and childcare not functioning and put in place welfare payments to try and boost the economy and at least stop people from going hungry during the outbreak.

In the medical world hospital casualties were divided into two areas- one part for treating the suspected coronavirus cases and the other for the regular patients with fractures etc. Staff were in full personal protective gear. The suspected coronavirus cases are processed, treated and if necessary, admitted to the covid-19 ward. There are no seats to sit on in this area and no drink is allowed in the corvid- 19 zones. The staff socially distance the 2 metres as much as possible and there is a social support line for corvid- 19 patients and for their relatives. Special arrangements are made for relatives in end-of-life situations and religious beliefs are catered for by the hospital chaplaincy services. Psychological assessments are done online and over the phone. Private hospitals have been leased by the H.S.E. to treat a variety of other illnesses not related to covid-19 during the crisis. Thankfully impossible choices have not had to be made so far regarding who gets a ventilator in an overcrowded situation.

In order to lessen the burden of lockdown there was plenty of advice out there. Get up at your usual time. Dress well in your best colourful clothes and it will make you feel good about yourself. Listen to the news once a day but do not get fixated on it. Constantly monitoring social media and unchecked sources can needlessly amplify anxiety and should be avoided. Moving, be it your 2-mile walk or around your back garden is important for your health and to get fresh air. Look out for your elderly neighbours. It is a great time to reflect on what you want from life. Write a book it could be a bestseller. In years to come you will wonder how you survived. Calendars are blank, no appointments, no work events, no markets, no bake sales, no choir practices, no weekends away, no book club, no sleepovers, maybe our garden bloomed and make up for it but one thing is certain we were blessed with fantastic weather at the beginning of the outbreak. One day of rain in 10 weeks during cocooning.

Co-watching movies with friends online. Cooking, quick naps, writing, drawing, painting, and numerous pursuits to keep you occupied. Dancing alone, running, and walking was highly recommended. Add to that patience, consideration, and kindness. Take breaks, read your books and play with the children. A dog can be a good addition as there is

plenty of time to train him, dogs trebled in price during the pandemic. Board games, a mini garden, video calls the list goes on.
Felicity raked out all the old photographs she had and did albums for all the family, the grandchildren herself and the weddings. This amounted to over 50 albums and took her 6 weeks. She attended to her small garden, cleaned the caravan until it was sparkling, and waited for the longed-for opening of the caravan park. Writing her book. interacting with grandchildren and looking out for the children's old nanny to make sure she was ok and her 101-year-old aunt in the nursing home. Life was never dull or lonely.

It was living alongside the brutal reality of this virus, the dying, the fear of loss, but there was something to look forward to with the gradual lifting of restrictions to eventually be able to get the hair done, all the grey roots, the split ends, the bushy-bearded hooded masses.

She seriously thought of getting a smoker to smoke fish but it didn't get off the ground. However, her son found an old bath down the field which he cleaned up and set up with blocks to make an outdoor tub which worked really well. She was lucky to have gathered seaweed last year and was able to use it to have a seaweed bath outdoors.

If sharing the house, divide your space to give some time alone to household members. Headphones and earplugs will help. There were reports of a spike in divorce applications and in domestic violence. Many aspired to become the top home school teachers.
Cars are obsolete, we cycle, we plant things we never thought of before. We meditate as a family, watch movies and play board games, it has been amazing how closeness to strangers has occurred. It is the long beginning of a certain end. Of course, there was the usual parade of jokes on whats app and on Viber and via email. Protect your valuables and a picture of a window full of toilet rolls, or a picture of a child with the last roll of toilet paper that granny got in 2020. Advice to fill your time in isolation by finishing things you had started and had only gotten halfway interpreted by some as finishing the bottles of whisky, brandy and gin left. In her daughter's hospital in the UK, staff were given forms to make a will if they so wished.

Children were coming and waving in the window to granny, they were not getting the virus but were thought to be carriers. Granny's house was out of bounds. Old people with co-morbidity started to pray again, these were the vulnerable. If you sneezed, coughed or got a temperature you rang the G.P. They sat in their confessionals arranging tests with the H.S.E., prescriptions for what they were not sure but were they not doing something.

They had gowns, gloves, and masks if you went to casualty. You parked in the car park outside the casualty. They came out in their space suits and brought you in in similar garb to investigate you i.e. chest x-ray, E.C.G , bloods, full examination but no swab for the virus as they only had a limited number of swabs,30 for a whole weekend. This was at the beginning of the pandemic. It's all about prioritising. This of course led to wild exaggeration of symptoms being unable to breathe, pains everywhere, severe chest problems, everything except the brown envelope to get treatment. You were put on a list for the test that would be 3 to 4 days, but you are still waiting a week later. And even if you get it it is taking 4 days to process it. Thankfully things improved as time progressed. What about contacts in the meantime if it is positive? This whole scenario changed with time to become much more efficient. Ireland has never seen anything like this before, the nearest being tuberculosis hidden and denied as a family disgrace but in fact, it was never as contagious as covid-19.

Cholera is another plague but the numbers were small. The covid- 19 was unprecedented in history. Felicity would say that when she was going for heart surgery she begged God to bring her through it and she would never complain again. That lasted for about 3 months then it was back to bickering, complaining and giving out. It's human nature. and so, it will be with this virus. Traditionally pandemics are blamed on far-away transmissions. This epidemic started in China and the rest of the world looked on critically as they fought to control it not thinking it would attack their own country. We knew about the sweating sickness in Italy in 1485 which brought a lucrative trade in holy medals. It was followed in 1630 by the bubonic plague, merry at breakfast and dead by noon.

It is typified by the economy shutting down, the vision of huge idle cranes at the warehouses, heaps of neglected carts, barrels and sacks in deserted cities. Covid-19 clarifies that the interconnectivity we enjoy in economic terms is also the vector that allows the disease to spread. How did we become a nation with over a thousand cases of covid-19? The patient reaching out to thank the doctor that he has made rich by his illness. One would think of Bram Stoker who invented Dracula and whose mother was from Sligo. He was influenced by the cholera epidemic. Epidemics like the coronavirus epidemic are great levellers attacking the prince and the pauper even Prince Charles was a victim of covid 19. Epidemics will turn the world upside down. The honest man will become a thief. The prostitute a saint, friends murderers and enemy's embrace. Note the huge increase in gun sales that occurred in America when coved 19 arrived in preparation for the time when food ran out.

One of the first casualties of the epidemic was Sunday and daily mass, the plague overcomes all obstacles and disregards boundaries until eventually all is turned into death. Many different opinions arise faced with death not least what should happen at funerals. Disrupting our way of life is one thing but preventing normal funeral rituals is another in Ireland, especially in the West where funerals occupy a priority stand. So, to sum up, what we have, is ghost cities, anxious people, isolation, and fear, The new world tells us how to teach, at home. How to entertain children, and how to shop online.

We are advised to set up food centres to cater to the medical people at the front line. Ring old friends, check in on neighbours, and cancel holidays. The new greeting is no longer, have a good day, but, keep safe. It is well known that Shakespeare wrote King Lear during the bubonic plague.
Let's look at another pandemic Cholera which caused headings in the papers, horror and death as Cholera strikes unleashing a nightmare of death in April 1832. Terror gripped the population as the dreaded news spread. It was a disease that struck suddenly. A family who had been visited at 9 am had six members dying twelve hours later. Carpenters were unable to keep up to the demand for coffins so many were buried

wrapped in pitched sheets and rolled into mass graves while rumours circulated of people being buried alive In the haste to dispose of the diseased body.   One doctor reported being called to a case but when he got there the hearse was already there. Tar barrels were lit at night to try and purify the air. Farmers avoided the towns and food became scarce..Townspeople who had a cow in their back garden shared milk with their neighbours but the empty jug had to be left out overnight and collected in the morning to be filled such was the fear of contact. In an effort to fumigate plates of salt with vitriolic acid were left outside windows and doors. In Sligo a small town the population fell from 15 thousand to 12 thousand giving a mortality rate of approx. 35 per cent What was different with Cholera was it was fast and furious. It eased off after six months. It was thought that its introduction to Sligo was due to people from Longford coming to avail of the sea bathing in Strandhill but the people who let lodging by the sea strongly denied it and threatened violence on the doctor that reported false facts. There was mass whitewashing and cleaning of houses. Nothing worked and Cholera became an overwhelming calamity. Attempts to open temporary hospitals were met with violent objections from the people living near leaving the health boards virtually helpless.

The harassing duties that fell to the medical men under these circumstances can be imagined but cannot be described. Doctors tried external and internal stimulants. Heat cold. Friction. Large and repeated doses of camolel. Opium, saline treatments, bleeding with leeches, wines and tonics. Such was the devastation that the provost of Sligo declared that he felt as if the end of the world had indeed come.

Now we have learned to live with covid19. The frequency and more importantly the severity has changed with multiple vaccinations got by the majority of the population. While still rampant it is generally now a mild disease causing no great distress but testing is still important and quarantine for one week if positive also we are encouraged to wear masks in crowds

It looks as if there will be yearly vaccinations against covid like the flu Travel has resumed with different restrictions in various countries.

Weddings and gatherings are taking place and the terror of covid has receded but that is not to say that there are still cases ending up in intensive care and dying. We must learn to live with it.

CHAPTER 12   MEDICAL INSIGHTS
****

After 20 years in general practice, you learn a few practical points and Felicity felt sorry for the worried well and the mums unable to make up their minds about their children's illnesses. Mark is sick, does he need a G.P. and be many euros lighter or can he be treated at home? So to highlight a number of practical points from the various specialities Felicity put pen to paper.

First, she felt children were the greatest mystery when it came to illness. There is the internet and google the bane of G. P.s life but the reality is too much information may make the parents even more worried. If Mark seems to be under the weather check is he eating or more telling is he refusing the smarties you are offering.? No interest in eating or drinking is a sign of trouble and this is especially relevant in babies under a year. Next, is he interested in his surroundings? heeding when someone walks into the room, playing with his toys, watching t v.If he is lying there responding to nothing wake him up and take heed. Is he vomiting? again wake up, other signs is a fast heart rate and you do not need to be a doctor to check this, count his pulse rate it should be below 80 beats per minute approx.

Is he complaining of abdominal pain? again note his gra for food. Get him to kick a ball with you. If it makes his pain worse it may be his appendix or again if he finds it hard going upstairs, Vomiting is another red light with abdominal pain. There is a condition called periodic abdominal pain which typically occurs in young females 7 to 14 and is a psychological illness. You may be suspect it if treats are not being refused or outings not turned down but sometimes it is very difficult to recognise it and the child genuinely feels the pain. Felicity will recount the story of the three-and-a-half-year-old who developed recurrent leg pain where she could not walk. After being in with the paediatrician in Sligo, having all the tests and then going to Dublin for a second opinion. where nothing was found to explain her symptoms. She came to Felicity on a Sunday carried in by the parents unable to walk. Felicity put her on the couch and examined her, assuring her that she knew what was wrong and that she would cure her and that it would never come back. Felicity got the patellar hammer and tapped her knee making her leg jump three times, told her she was cured and to get off the couch and walk out which she did and that was the end of it.

Allergy testing is of limited use in children but if you have a specific severe allergy like eggs it may respond to desensitisation. In an acute allergy, it is important to always carry an EpiPen, there should be one in the house, one in the car, and one in the school, it may be a life saver. It may be well worth desensitising them to a specific allergy keeping in mind that this may take up to twelve or fourteen injections. It is not practical with multiple allergies. so just to recap. with children vomiting only serious with lethargy, fever and off their food. Try treats to see if they are genuine.

Cough - wait and watch. If the chest is not wheezy they should get over it in a week, after this, you need to use common sense. Temperature - usually due to infection of the throat or ears, will settle in a few days with Calpol. Pain-if in the ear, it will need an antibiotic as repeated ear infections with ruptured ear drums may cause deafness.
Felicity will talk about the probiotic brigade. The first time she was asked about biopics she said she did not know what they were while thinking to herself new aged rubbish, Another favourite of the new-age enlightened parent is to ban all dairy products and typically the same brigade will enquire where they can get allergy testing done for their child. Allergy

testing will usually be positive for seven to eight substances. It takes eighteen injections to desensitise to one substance. People are cashing in on allergy testing, especially in America. They give the patient a substance to hold e.g. nuts and then claim that by checking their heart rate, and colour. respiratory rate etc. they can tell if they are allergic to the product.

Another modern myth is the numbers that are thought to be allergic to gluten are diagnosed without any tests whatsoever and so are started on gluten-free diets without any proper diagnosis of coeliac disease which is the only reason to exclude gluten from their diets. Look at the shelves in any supermarket, they are full of gluten-free products even though coeliac is a rare disease. Turn down the central heating, and put it off at night. Bugs thrive in heat; You must have heard the old people saying that a good fall of snow would get rid of the bugs.

Everyone knows that headaches and a rash especially in a child are not to be taken lightly, do not delay even by 10 minutes, it makes a difference in pneumococcal or meningococcal meningitis.
Diarrhoea - a common condition in children and one that can cause dehydration and severe illness if ignored, A few home truths, they lose sodium and potassium with the diarrhoea, these are to be found in seven up and in coca cola so no solids and plenty seven up or coca cola, Jonnie is starving and is begging for something to eat, you are so delighted he is getting better so you renege on no solids and just give him a slice of toast and you are right back to square one. Did you ever hear about being cruel to be kind? You better learn.

If you are one of the mums that raise their hands in horror at fizzy drinks you can get dioralyte sachets across the counter from the chemist to make a more scientific drink to replace the sodium and potassium but the secret is no solids. Going to the doctor is a major event but nothing like it was years ago. Going round in your head is the thought, does he think I am a fool with the questions I ask? Is he concerned? It's a merry-go-round. This is an attempt to take common scenarios and try to establish a light-hearted but expert approach to them without boring people to death with words of wisdom.

Remember you know your own child better than anyone else and if you are still worried after the doctor has reassured you seek a second opinion. Felicity will recount how a traveller's family came to her house with the baby after they had seen the consultant in the hospital as they were still worried and how proud she was that they had such faith in her, a humble G.P. How she reassured them. Some months later she met them again and inquired after the baby to be told that after they left her they went to Castlebar hospital and were seen by another consultant. A baby hot and twitching is a danger zone. Strip the infant and tepid sponge the whole body, there is nothing more frightening than a convulsing baby so G.P. is the next stop and Felicity will tell you that you are not the only one afraid, G.Ps are also afraid of convulsions. As regards the respiratory system rapid breathing or even worse, grunting is an emergency and Felicity will talk of the two worst cases she had which both ended up in I.C.U in Crumlin but thankfully survived.

If there is a family history of squints ie strabismus get your child checked early at two years even though it may not be evident as it needs to be corrected in childhood or will leave a weak eye.

The end of childhood varies and is debatable but do you as a parent realise the power your children have for example "I am not going to school and you can't make me" what do you do? you cannot carry them into school protesting, and you can't give them a good slap but you are responsible for them and you may be fined for not having them at school. They may complain you to the authorities if you lay a hand on them. If they break up the house, you are still obliged legally to give them protection.

A lot of satisfaction and reward comes from treating children as they generally respond but you can get caught out as Felicity will relate how she sent a two-year-old to the hospital who was passing frank red urine but failed to ask if he had eaten any beetroot which will give you red urine. Most medics will tell you that sick children scare them the most and rightly so. If you were a vet your subject could never tell you what they were complaining of just like children. Felicity was terrified of doctors when she was a child and had to be carried into school medicals kicking and crying and one would wonder if it was this fear that drove her on to do medicine. A perverse way of overcoming the captive. When the great gurus of medicine i.e. --medical consultants proclaim the way forward you listen and then you do the work.

How medicine has changed for the better there is no doubt with access to google, articles, media and education with a public proactive regarding health. Sometimes too proactive as per G.Ps.
Exercise is the basis for good health both physical and mental. Basically, the best is walking and it's free. Everyone knows this but not everyone takes exercise. We are exhausted by evening time and can't contemplate going out, it's too cold, it's too late, it's too dangerous, the family needs quality time with you, it's raining, and the list goes on.
Ever stop to think about the Germans, they have the right coats, the proper shoes and the proper headwear so the weather is not an issue. This was very evident to Felicity on her deep sea fishing trips, Germans with the right bait, the right clothes, the right equipment, whereas the Irish will have the wrong shoes , clothes e t c except that these tall manly Germans are prone to seasickness and as Felicity would admit a slight satisfaction she would feel when they are puking over the side of the boat. Pity they can't command their stomachs as well as their other bits and bobs but one must hand it to them on their organisational skills. Felicity did an exchange with a German family's children for five years, her children going out to Germany for a month and the German family coming back for a month and it was a very positive experience both from a discipline perspective in so much as her children had to take their shoes off at the door, no going to the fridge after 6 o'clock, sitting down to family meals and waiting until everyone was finished whereas when the German children came back they appreciated the ability to graze all day, watch TV when they wanted, cycle all around the countryside and go camping. The family they went to were called Estherhausey and was an old aristocratic family with famous musicians in their past. There was one girl in the family and when she came she spilled all the beans about Felicity's daughter being brought to a banquet in a castle and plonking herself down at the banquet table and diving into the starters that were on the table before grace was said or anyone else was seated.

Sophie, as she was called, said that her parents were worried that anyone would do anything to her on her Irish visit but Felicity reassured her that no one here would bother her. Sophie had her pocket money of 20 euros for 3 weeks and wanted to spare it as the boys had spent all their pocket money when they came. Some of us could take a leaf out of their book.

To get back to the exercise where there is a will there is a way. Get up a half hour earlier so that you have your exercise every day. You could try leaving the milk scarce so you have to go and get it or if you left for work twenty minutes earlier you could get a cheaper car park and walk from there to work. If your work involves waiting for people, get an extra key for the transport so your passengers have access to your car, and you can do your walk. What about your lunch break is it an hour, half an hour eating and half an hour walking? Could you rekindle romance by drawing hubby out for a night walk under the stars, even study the stars and sharing the experience? It takes a bit of planning, but everyone can fit in half an hour a day to walk. If all fails, there is the treadmill used in most houses that have one for hanging clothes on. So now you are walking tra la la.

Felicity swears that nothing will keep your joints oiled as well as swimming. Swimming is a great exercise as it has a social element as well as being particularly good for your joints and general mobility. Nowadays there are swimming pools and gyms in every small town. Felicity remembers going on holiday and the hotel had a swimming pool where she got talking to a number of elderly members who told her how they were scheduled for surgery on their knees but after joining the leisure centre and swimming they were able to cancel their surgery.

Next, we come to eating and weight. The concept is so simple: do not eat and you lose weight, it costs you nothing and you save money. People are making a fortune out of fat people from surgeons doing bariatric surgery to the five-star gyms popping up all over the island. Who cares that you are fat, the doctors will say it's good for business, Your nearest and dearest will appreciate the good hold he can get on you but will be less inclined to parade you on the social occasions. The shops will love you so no one but you can do anything about it. The concept is so simple, do not eat and you lose weight, it costs you nothing and you save money.

After years of G.P. practise what works for weight loss? Keep it simple, one plan is to cut out all the bread. Replace it with fruit and cracker bread in the long yellow boxes. Felicity uses these cracker bread with stewed apple which she makes herself and sweetens it with artificial sweetener. She has cracker breads, four in the morning with the apple and hummus. It must be something you like, non-fattening and stick to it, it can also be used as a snack. Have raw carrots ready in the fridge and maybe raw celery, cucumber is another option, it must be things you like, and they must be ready to eat, prepared in other words. If you take sugar in your tea, look how much sugar you use a day by putting the spoonfuls you use in a cup, it may be over half full by nighttime, use artificial sweeteners. Support may be necessary such as weight watchers or a dietician often good to motivate as you will be going back you will be anxious to please everyone as well as yourself. If you do not eat you get thin full stop. After years of practice you get used to hearing I eat practically nothing and can't lose weight; it's my nature to be fat, rubbish forget it. These are the time wasters.

Now you are walking, swimming and losing weight. You are three-quarters of the way to healthy living provided you do not smoke. If you do give them up, get a child's dummy and suck it instead or use nicotine chewing gum. After 40 years in practice, it's the greatest killer of all affecting the throat, heart, lungs, liver and gastric system.

Here there is no contest. Go to an uninhabited island with a bag of apples, a tent and the bare necessities, tell the boatman to come back in 3 weeks at which stage you will be cured of the habit and may even have lost weight as well.

When all is said and done joining a gym will fulfil the exercise, the swimming, and do wonders for your social life. Where better to have a chat than in your togs surrounded by water, steam etc? There is something liberating about it. A friend of Felicity who was a psychologist said her love of swimming was a desire to get back into the womb. This might be true and hopefully, she would bond with her mother better the second time around.

What about cholesterol, it's mainly a genetic problem rather than a dietary one much and all as the commercial world would tell you otherwise. Stop worrying about it, stop buying all these special foods that you were never taught how to cook, get your cholesterol checked every 3 to 4 years and if it is under 6 stop worrying about it. The stress will put it up and trying to remember when to go to the doctor. and having the money to pay will depress you.

Many patients would complain to Felicity about the side effects of statins that are used to control cholesterol. They do have side effects but the invisible damage that cholesterol does clogging up the arteries is worse than the side effects so do not read the blurb on the medication and remember it's only one in ten that will have side effects, usually the fussy ones and the so-called well-informed.

When all is said and done what is necessary
1 breast checks every 3 years
2 prostate checks after 45 with yearly bloods
3 colonoscopies every 2 years if there is a family history of colon cancer
4 blood pressure check yearly

Set aside one agony day a year to visit your G.P. and get all done and presuming that you have no symptoms forget it for another year. A word of warning on blood pressure is a silent destroyer of kidneys and heart, your local pharmacy will do it for you. Osteoporosis is a silent creeper like the blue clematis plant. It sinks its tentacles into you so think of it at least every 3 years after 60 as it can be stopped in its tracks. They now have an injection for osteoporosis called protea which will prevent it from advancing.

What about flu and pneumococcal infection? Excommunicate both by getting the flu and the pneumococcal vaccine. What is the worst that can happen if you do not get the vaccines, wait for it, pneumococcal meningitis, septicaemia, organ failure and dialysis for the rest of your life if you survive it? Who would not have the simple prod.? This is what happened to Felicity's husband when he was in his seventies making his last years miserable.

You will hear talk of vitamins like B12 or levels of calcium and vitamin D . They need to be checked once after the age of 60 and then forgotten about for another 3 years unless they are abnormal. Vitamin D is obtained from the sun, calcium from eggs and milk, and vitamin B from meat and greens so a good diet and plenty of fresh air. Remember the humble nettle. It is full of vitamins, add it to soup and the dandelions all over your lawn they are packed with nutrients add them to soups and to salads.

Headaches and dizziness, do you go to a quack no it's a docs case and do not delay. There have been complaints of dizziness, nausea, and vomiting, circulating for the past ten years due to probably a virus which is treated with a drug called stemetil.
The hospital diagnoses it as vestibulitis which is due to a virus infection of the vestibular bone in the middle ear. Because teenagers are sensitive to stemetil if treated they may develop severe staggering with nystagmus and look sinister. Normally no one knows what is wrong with them but it is the extrapyramidal effects of the stemetil and will settle down over twelve hours with no long-term harm. Felicity had two of these cases and in the first one she rushed to the hospital where they were equally puzzled, the second one she took in her stride as she knew what it was. What are the two problems doctors hate to hear about, back pain and I cannot sleep? Felicity tells them that want of sleep never killed anyone so that was one problem solved. Sleeping on a hard surface, like a thin mattress with a board under it, is better than an orthopaedic mattress for back pain.

Get them to take up swimming but all may be of limited benefit. Not worth a dam as one man described the advice, so surgery is the next stop. Surgery is the final step, there are no more options, remember the old spinal cord is lurking around the spinal area so not to be undertaken lightly.

Felicity would maintain that the single biggest factor that affects health is activity or a lack of it closely followed by obesity. It's why there are so many widows and so few widowers. The widowers are preparing an early grave by resting to improve their health. With the dawn of wearing a watch that tells you how many steps you take per day the real difference shows up between men and women.

Back in the modern age and now abortion is on demand up to 9 weeks of pregnancy. Maybe we should say killing on demand for up to 9 weeks. Better if one could go the full term and have the child adopted. You will have saved a life but also given some couple endless joy, a reason to live, the greatest gift that money cannot buy. Are you selfless enough? It would be a huge sacrifice on your part. If there are foetal abnormalities, it's another story and abortion is the way forward.

What about euthanasia? Think how we treat old dogs that are in pain, we get them put down. Well-regulated euthanasia is a merciful service to alleviate physical and mental anguish should the patient wish it and provided the proper controls are put in place.

If things go wrong should you sue the doctor? 99% of doctors do not set out to deliberately harm you. They see 20 to 40 patients a day five days a week. That is over 150 patients a week. They will make an odd mistake, it's inevitable. For some reason, it will tear them apart to be sued, think about it first and talk to them about it. They may encourage you to proceed if the mistake has caused significant morbidity. They have insurance and that is what it is for but do not leave them and vilify them from afar. They have feelings too you know and they do lie awake often wondering if your Johnnie who they treated earlier will be all right or not, wondering should they have sent him to the hospital or the breast they examined and found no lump but it was a large fibrocystic breast and difficult to be sure. A person is not like the engine of your car. By missing something you may condemn them to a life of torture. Doctors need partners and colleagues to unload their worries and anxieties onto. Due to the confidentiality clause, it's limited who they can speak to. Priests have a confidentiality clause, but they cannot do you any harm from the other side of the grid in confession. Felicity has seen good honest caring colleagues ruined due to legal cases taken against them so much so that some of them never work again.

Jealousy is a common finding among the public concerning doctors. They are perceived as being loaded financially a myth if ever there was one. They have multiple expenses including secretaries, nurses, equipment, travel expenses and huge insurance costs   Straight away you can half what they get. Added to this the pension is abysmal, something that is never mentioned in the media when they print the doctor's salaries.
Their lifestyle puts pressure on their home life, stress levels are high, and expectations are higher than expected from other professionals so G.P. is not for the faint-hearted.

Enough of the downside, jobs are plentiful, diversity is possible, they can become trainers of young G.Ps, work in a hospital, teach and many more openings. They meet people every day and make great bonds with many which is a very rewarding part of medicine. They earn the respect of others, have a good lifestyle and finally can improve people's lives and work into old age provided the dreaded Alzheimer's does not strike. What about mental health? When you feel down try and change your lifestyle to get a better life for yourself. Take one night a week out to something you enjoy like art classes or what interests you. Activities that you could do during the day if you are a stay-at-home mum, computer classes, language classes, charity work, yoga anything that gets you out of the house and interacting with others. If all fails and remember to avoid the alcohol it is a depressant, then go to your G.P. As the modern antidepressants are mild, not addictive and very effective especially combined with cognitive behavioural therapy and exercise. There is light at the end of the tunnel

CHAPTER THIRTEEN RETIREMENT
****

Felicity would expound on retirement, a sad day or an opportunity to do other things. It's both of those things. Keep hens, get a dog he will make you exercise, the hens will give you eggs but you must feed them and clean out their shed. Form a bond with your grandchildren, feed them two evenings a week and you are guaranteed access on those days. Go to horse racing, your choices are endless. Get a hot tub. Felicity got a plumber who brought a hot tap out onto her patio. She sourced a good second-hand bath and the bath was plumed to the drainage and fitted under the hot tap. She then gathered the proper seaweed in Rosses point and enjoyed many seaweed baths out under the sun, rain and snow. That in a nutshell is what will keep you healthy and give you a long life. You could try changing your life, go to a different supermarket, or attend a different church. Join a gym. Going back to education, it's endless what one can do. Books are a lifeline. Join a book club and meet once or twice a month. Look after others belonging to you but do not volunteer to babysit on a permanent basis, be there for emergencies if the babysitter has a wedding or the child is sick. As a granny, it will give you a chance to mother and guide a child without the stress of motherhood so enjoy every minute of it. Lastly, why not write a book

When Felicity retired, she kept up her registration with the medical council which meant she could do locums for other GPs. There is something exciting about going into other doctors' surgeries to hold the fort for them, meet new staff, see another method of practice and help colleagues out. The secretary of one of the locums Felicity did greet her with the words   I was awake all night wondering what I would do with you a worry that Felicity quickly put to rest. When eventually the surgery was quiet, and she had seen everyone she heard whistling, so she thought someone else came in but when she went out there was no one there . She was not long back until the whistling started again, this time she crept out silently and discovered it was the secretary that was whistling all the time.

Another colleague rang to book her on a Friday but did not say where he was going. Later she heard he had taken off to get married. Two weeks later he contacted her for cover again and she asked him if he was getting divorced but got silence on the other end. Some people have no sense of humour.

On the locum scene, Felicity was anxious to get a regular slot and this became possible in an adjoining practice seven miles from her. She worked there on a regular basis, got to know the patients, the staff were dependable, she was punctual and committed.

Felicity had enjoyed a long and happy time in her own practice for 41 years and she was lucky to be popular and made many friends but that changed when she did locums as many of the patients wanted their own doctor and often left to come back another day. Felicity would say it was good for the soul.

After 6 years in this practice, she went to the next town to work for a male single-handed practitioner. Had a very happy 2 to 3 years there as well as making good friends with the secretary. On these locums, she found great walks like Lough Talt and the football pitch in Gurteen. Unfortunately, covid put an end to the locums as did the medical insurance who wanted seven and a half thousand euros to do one day a week.

CHAPTER 14 EPILOGUE
****

On that note Felicitys advice is to do everything you can possibly do to keep going and seal your longevity.

From Donegal's misty hills and sea,
Fair Felicity grew up wild and free,
In Portnablagh's fishing village quaint,
Where life was simple, and love was saint.
Boarding school opened up her mind,
And medicine's call was hard to hide,
At U.C.D., she studied with the boys,
And her heart brimmed with ambitious joys.
From Scotland to America's shore,
Felicity honed her healing lore,
And in Sligo, she made her stand,
A GP of great repute in the land.
Love found her in Sligo's verdant glades,
A dream home, a family, and love cascades,
Horses were her husband's noble craft,
Their life together, a happy, loving draft.
But fate, alas, has a cruel way,
And in 2016, her love did pass away,
Felicity travelled the world with friends,
Her heart on her sleeve, love that never ends.
Through Covid's trials, she stood tall,
Her spirit unbowed, her heart a thrall,
From the cradle to infinity's call,
Felicity's life, a Yeatsian thrall.

Printed in Great Britain
by Amazon